# TABLE OF CONTENTS

# The Farmer and the Grill

## A GUIDE TO GRILLING, BARBECUING AND SPIT-ROASTING GRASSFED MEAT

*... and for saving the planet,
one bite at a time.*

**Shannon Hayes,**
author of *The Grassfed Gourmet Cookbook*

Foreword by **Joel Salatin**

left
to
write
PRESS

The Farmer and the Grill
A Guide to Grilling, Barbecuing
and Spit-Roasting Grassfed Meat
by Shannon Hayes

Published by Left to Write Press
270 Rossman Valley Road
Richmondville, NY 12149
www.grassfedcooking.com
518-827-7595

First Edition Paperbook
Copyright © 2007 Shannon Hayes

Cataloging-in-Publication Data has been filed with the Library of Congress.

ISBN 978-0-9794391-0-0
ISBN 0-9794391-0-8

Illustrations by Robert Hooper
Design by Carol Clement

Printed in the USA

10  9  8  7  6  5  4  3  2  1

# Acknowledgments

No girl learns to grill on an island. I owe thanks to countless folks, and now's the test to see how many of them I can list:

First and foremost, my thanks go to that couple who bought that first sirloin steak in 2004 at the farmers' market, then ruined it because I wasn't able to tell them how to grill it. Sorry if I caused a rift in your marriage. I hope you're still together.

Next, thanks are due my friend Aissa O'Neil of Betty Acres Farm, editor of the NOFA-NY newsletter, who sweetly asked me a few years back to write an article on cooking grassfed meat. In an ornery mood that day, I told her "no." Sorry I was rude, Aissa, and thanks for politely refusing my refusal. Because that turned into the first grilling article, which then turned into this book.

Next, I owe a mountain of gratitude to the extended families in Argentina—to the men who spent hours in the heat of summer divulging their secrets before the flames; to the women who taught me their recipes and welcomed Bob, Saoirse and me into their homes; and to the children, friends, neighbors and dining companions who offered their educated critiques of every morsel of grilled meat, honing my palate with every bite. Thanks go to the Zerolinis: Oscar, Gonzalo, Nancy, Santiago, Emiliano, Matías, Griselda Cornaló, Norberto, Irene, Leticia, Germán, Cármen Zampedri, Julián and Esteban Rodriquez, Mabel Dalprá, Gabriela, Carina, Alejandra, Andrés and Paula; and to Delicia, *abuela* to us all. Thanks also to the Dalzottos: Toto, Valeria, Carlos and Ester Zerolini. And most especially, I owe my thanks to La Familia Gomez. I was nineteen when you first took me in to your home, and had never given much thought to the food on my plate before I sat at your kitchen table and out in your *quincho*. I thank you for your love, patience, guidance and boundless generosity over the last fourteen years. My kitchen shelves are weighed down from years of cookbook collecting, but my countertop remains covered with the pages of the notes I took while living with you. When the tastes and smells of your kitchen are evoked in my own, I feel we are still together. My heart forever belongs to you—to Néstor, Graciela, Guillermo and Laura, Guille and Ana Rios, and to the most enduring, best friend a *gringa* could ever hope for, Sonia Gomez.

And now for a few more American *amigos*: Thank you to Coleen O'Shea for your enthusiasm for the project and to Fran McManus and Wendy Rickard of Eating Fresh Publications for your constant support and friendship. Thanks to Carol Clement and Steve Hoare for your help bringing this book to publication; and to Susan McGiver and Harva Corporation for adding even more life to the project. Thank you to Ginny and Victor Guyer, who bought us our Weber kettle. Thank you to Frank Davis, who stepped up to the plate (and grill) for recipe testing when I developed an aversion to pork during my first trimester. Thanks also to Cherie Davis of Chaoskitty for her ingenious website design.

Thank you to Troy Bishopp, "The Grass Whisperer," whose enthusiasm for my work has a way of taking me to the right people at the right time. The day after I decided to nail the coffin shut on this book and abandon the project, Troy took me to Greg Judy, author of *No Risk Ranching*. In a few minutes of conversation, Greg emphasized the need for the work and gave me the energy I needed to keep going. Thanks go to Jo Robinson, author of *Pasture Perfect*, for your years of friendship, your wise counsel, your business savvy and your idea to self-publish. Thank you to Joel Salatin for your encouragement and your inspiration.

Thanks, once more, to my folks, Jim and Adele Hayes, the head honchos at Sap Bush Hollow Farm. They support my meat habit, my kid habit, my writing habit.

Thank you to Bob, my husband, who patiently stood at the coals when morning sickness kept me away, who photographed our adventures, edited my manuscripts, and freed me in every way possible to do my work.

And thank you to Saoirse, my daughter, who journeyed to eight different countries and three different continents before her third birthday, keeping Mommy and Daddy company as they worked. You bore the brunt of the travel ailments and still maintained your vivacious spirit; you opened doors for us with your infectious smiles and coy linguistic talents; and you made friends wherever you went. And you kid-tested every one of these recipes. I'm proud of you, I'm thankful for your company, and I love you. Gratitude also goes to kid number two, who kicks in my belly as I write. You, too, endured an awful lot of grilling and barbecue while in gestation. May your journey into this world be safe, healthy, happy and flavorful.

*This book is dedicated to the grass farmers of North America. I have cherished every word of encouragement you have ever offered; I've saved every e-mail, every card, every note scratched on the side of an order form; I've relished every phone call, and every conversation. Your support has meant the world to me. You are bastions of hope for our communities and for our planet. Every word of this text was written with you in mind. Thank you for all you are doing.*

# FOREWORD

## Joel Salatin, Polyface Farm

"Oh, so that's how you do it," escaped my lips for the umpteenth time as a sudden "Aha" permeated my frontal lobe while I read the first draft of Shannon Hayes' *The Farmer and the Grill*. All of us who have struggled with grilling nuances on our pastured meats and poultry will find this handbook/cookbook both liberating and empowering.

As a quintessential devotee of pastured livestock, I am keenly aware that the most environmentally-progressive meat and poultry in the world will not sell unless the eater has a favorable dining experience. At the end of the day, taste and eating pleasure trump altruism every time. Healing the planet and keeping cancer at bay just don't compare to the visceral bond connecting nose, palate, and pocketbook.

Within the pastured livestock movement, many voices, often preceded by the word "expert," offer advice for producing a product with handling qualities identical to those substances coming out of Concentrated Animal Feeding Operations. I call them substances because compared to their grass-based counterparts, the nutrient-dense edible portions are merely substances. They taste bland, feel flaccid, and handle slovenly.

But pasture-based meat and poultry bursts with flavor, expresses muscle tone, and handles with integrity. And that's just what you can sense. Beyond that are the myriad nutritional values; and beyond that are a host of ecological, emotional, and economic factors screaming "This is the right way!" to pastured livestock. We applaud differences.

Too many of us producing these products, however, are being counseled to make them mimic conventional fare. And that sells our noble alternative short. But few things are as ingrained in the human psyche as cooking. We have preconceptions and notions of how things are supposed to be. We all like consistency.

Shannon, bless her, has brought to our collective tables an action plan to celebrate differences. She doesn't even take issue with charcoal lovers vs. propane grill hotshots, but patiently wades through the differences so that all of us, in our fundamental routines, can adapt to the exciting new qualities offered through pastured meats.

These meats, of course, will express farm individualities. From breed to climate to grass variety to time of year, these highly individualized and localized meats offer discoveries that keep them ever new.

Now, armed with *The Farmer and the Grill*, all of us marketing these land-healing meats can confidently embrace our customers with customized instructions. Ultimately, our farm's individuality lands on someone's plate. Our batting average for home runs just went way up. Thank you, Shannon.

# Introduction

## A Girl Meets Her Grill

Mine was the loneliest little Weber on the planet. A generous house-warming gift from friends, I rolled it outside, then mentally relegated that sweet little kettle to my husband's world, nestled somewhere between his case of motor oil and his power tools.

He didn't agree with that placement. Knowing my passion for all things food, he felt this little Weber and I were unacknowledged soul mates, destined to meet and enrich each others' lives. He tried numerous times to coax me out to the coals, to encourage me to get friendly with the fire. But I repeatedly brushed him off, insisting that grills and barbecues were the man's domain. I dared not cross the gender threshold and risk wreaking havoc on a happy marriage. The grill was his, the oven was mine.

Which is not to say I didn't think about it. A lot. I loved the look of that barbecue...the sensuous curves, the feel of the handle, the way the shiny surface caught the light of the summer sun and reflected back fish-eye images of my life: our garden, our daughter tumbling with the dog, the guinea hens scampering across the yard after them. On occasion I would reach out as I walked across our patio to run my hand along its smooth surface.

I wanted to enter this world, to understand about fire and wood, about working with the flavors of smoke and using it to create magic with great meat. But I was intimidated by it. I didn't know how to light a grill, much less how to manage a flame.

I had tasted great grassfed barbecue, slow-cooked by talented pit masters, and I knew the power of it. Unlike industrially produced meat, barbecued pastured pork can make the most stoic of men return to long lost childhoods in the deep south, evoking more emotions and tears than a session in psychoanalysis. I've watched perfectly grilled grassfed steaks cause the most hard-to-please gourmets to set down their knives and forks, pause in their feasts and say, "Oh, my God. I've never tasted anything so good."

Honoring such power, I opted to respect my backyard Weber, allowing it to glow in its own mystique, rather than risk a gastronomic catastrophe tantamount to the calamities evoked when the Sorcerer's Apprentice overstepped his bounds. But one day, not long ago, all that changed.

It was our first day selling our meats at the Pakatakan Farmers' Market in Margaretville, New York. A married couple approached us, eager to sample a grassfed steak. I talked to them about how to cook it on the stove, and then the man said that they intended to grill it. With no advice to offer on that subject, I packed their meat up and sent them on their way, wishing them the best of luck.

The next week, only the woman returned. And she was furious with me. She and her husband were fighting. The costly grilled meat was terrible, they were not speaking and, implicitly, I was to blame.

I was humiliated. But worse, I thought of all the work my family had invested producing that steak. My father had carefully selected the genetics and stewarded those animals across our pastures for nearly two years, studying their growth and muscle development daily, working to keep them calm and happy. We'd dry-aged the meat and scrupulously examined the marbling. To be told our meat was terrible after all the love and labor we'd invested was heartbreaking. I returned home that day with a heavy heart, poured myself a drink, then sat out on the patio and puzzled over what could have gone wrong. I looked up for a moment and saw the answer reflected back at me in that little Weber. If I was going to represent my family's business at the Pakatakan Farmers' Market during grilling season, it was time that the Weber and I got to know each other. I couldn't let another customer fall upon bad advice and ruin the fruits of our labors.

And so began my next Odyssey into the world of grilling grassfed meat. As I had done in writing *The Grassfed Gourmet*, I learned to cook every piece of meat we produced on our farm, but this time using my little Weber as both a grill and a barbecue. This was not an easy challenge. To grill and barbecue requires more understanding and interaction with the meat and the flames than using a precisely calibrated oven. If it is cold outside, you must make adjustments. If it is windy, you must accommodate for that as well. For the most part, there are no pans to insulate your food from the heat source. Then, add to the equation grassfed and pastured meats, which are sometimes leaner, more variable and have more pronounced muscle tissue and robust full flavor. It is radically different from the industrially produced meat most of us are used to. There was much to learn.

The Odyssey quickly became an obsession that pulled me away from the confines of my backyard. In order to better understand the world of meat, we began taking trips. We went down south to see real pit masters in action. We traveled to Europe, where legs of lamb, beef roasts and chickens turned on spits in the windows of little restaurants. For three months we made our home in France, befriending local butchers, observing their cuts, tasting their meats. We didn't stop there. Every pasture farmer has heard lore about Argentina, the Mecca for grilled grassfed beef, and so we made a pilgrimage down to South America, where we practiced with the *asadores* to refine our craft even further. And naturally, all along the way, we met farmers—all of them loving their land, their livestock, and great food.

This book chronicles our greatest lessons from this Odyssey. It is filled with easy recipes and tips for grilling, barbecuing and spit-roasting great grassfed and pastured meats. Further, it offers essays on the heroic role each of us plays in preserving our culture, our land, and our culinary traditions simply by making a commitment to choose and cook good, wholesome food for our families.

I've been known to grow misty-eyed when I talk about the synergy between sustainable farming, the world's greatest food and the health of our planet, about the sanctity of our earth's soils, and our responsibility to steward them properly. This book is yet another testimonial to these ideals. Whether you are a man or woman, a grilling greenhorn or a pit-master pro, there is a wide world of great food experiences awaiting you once you step outside and lay a piece of grassfed meat across the grate. I hope to take you there with the coming pages so that together, with our local farmers, we can work to save the planet, one delicious bite at a time.

CHAPTER ONE

# From Grass to the Grill

If this is your first foray into the world of grassfed and pastured meats, welcome. If you are a "seasoned" meat connoisseur, welcome back.

All the wonderful news about grassfed meat has finally begun to take hold. When we first began selling pasture-raised lamb, beef, pork and poultry, it seemed that every new prospective customer required an introduction to the many benefits of raising animals on grass. We lectured nonstop about why keeping animals out in the fields—rather than confined to a feedlot—was not only more humane, but also better for the environment and the consumer. Raising animals on pasture and marketing them directly helps ensure the environmental and financial sustainability of small farms like ours, and keeps valuable agricultural businesses thriving in our community. It contributes to local food security by guaranteeing availability of wholesome, clean food, with relatively little impact from the larger world's troubles. The viability of our business means that we can afford to continue farming our beautiful land, rather than being forced to sell it to a developer to carve into housing lots. Best of all, we can assure people that this meat is decidedly safer and more healthful to eat.

Today, we hardly have to explain anything. Even our new customers are so well-informed about the benefits of small-scale sustainable farming, the importance of keeping livestock on pasture, and the hazards of factory-farmed foods that now they are teaching *us*, sharing articles, news clips and research reports with every visit.

Among the many glories of being a grassfed meat producer is that the good news about our work just keeps coming. We were pleased when we learned that grassfed meat was a source of omega-3 fatty acids, which have been linked to blood pressure reduction, healthy brain function and the slowed growth of many types of cancer. We were thrilled when research showed that products such as ours were also a source of conjugated linoleic acids, or CLAs, which preliminary research has linked to improved immune systems and lowered risk of cancer and heart disease (1), earning it the moniker "the cancer-fighting fat." We were elated to learn that grassfed meat was much less likely to be contaminated with the virulent strain of *E.coli* O157:H7 (2,3), and ecstatic when studies showed grassfed meat contains antioxidant vitamins.

All this research emerged a few years ago. Yet even today, the positive findings just keep coming. A July 2005 report released by the USDA Agricultural Research Service showed that properly managed pastures were able to store two to three times more carbon in their soil than fields that were left unmanaged, used for hay, or left unharvested. While carbon dioxide is critical to sustain life on this planet, excessive atmospheric carbon contributes to the greenhouse effect (4). Another study released by Iowa State University shows similar findings, indicating that grazed pasture is the ideal land use for storing carbon (5). Simply put, raising animals on well-managed pasture helps to reverse the greenhouse effect. The USDA report also shows that proper grazing management helps preserve topsoil, reminding us that when we farm in harmony with Mother Nature, our health, our communities, and our planet will continue to reap the benefits.

In a world fraught with environmental degradation, withering rural communities, social inequities, chronic illness and declining food quality, it seems safe to say that we can each begin to have an impact on restoring our personal and planetary health simply by thoughtfully choosing the food we eat. Selecting grassfed meat is a fantastic beginning.

### How to know you're getting the real thing

With so much good news about raising animals on grass, there has to be a "catch" someplace. And there is. As grassfed meat has grown in popularity, many companies are touting "pseudo-grass-fed" products, using clever names and labels that dupe consumers into thinking they are buying the real thing, when in truth, they're still getting industrially grown, factory-farmed meat. Some of the potentially misleading words employed are "all natural," "free-range," "prairie-raised"—the list goes on and on. Of course, many *legitimate* pasture-based producers use these same terms as genuine descriptions of the work they are doing. But increasingly, there are a number of industrial meat companies that use these ambiguous terms on their labels, capitalizing on consumers' growing concerns about the problems associated with factory farming. Such corporations, to hold their market share against the tide of consumers' health awareness and social consciousness, engage in creative, albeit misleading, marketing ploys to achieve their aims.

In order for grassfed products to truly deliver the benefits described above, lamb and beef must be *completely grass-fed*. Poultry and pigs are omnivores, which means they will require some grain in their diet, but they, too, should still be *pastured,* out roaming the fields. Once you've experienced true grassfed and pastured meat flavors, your palate should be able to tell you when you've been snookered. Grassfed and pastured meats will be firm, not mushy; their respective meat flavors will be more pronounced. Still, it takes time to be able to readily recognize the flavor and texture differences.

Until then, Jo Robinson, creator of Eatwild.com, and author of *Pasture Perfect*, insists that the only way to know for sure is to seek out the producers themselves. She encourages consumers to call the phone numbers on the meat packages of meat claiming to be grassfed (6). Ask specifically where the animals are raised, what they are fed, and how they are managed.

Most importantly, ask what these animals are fed in the final weeks of their lives. Animals that are primarily raised on grass, but then finished on grain, lose the nutritional, environmental and social benefits that pure grassfed meat offers.

Finally, ask if you can visit the farm. Provided you are respectful of their time and busy schedule, legitimate pasture-based farmers will usually welcome your visit to see their operation. An industrially based factory farm will not.

Better still, try to buy your meat directly from the farmer. Pasture-based farms sell their products at farmers' markets all across the country. Many of them are also listed in the farmer directory at Eatwild.com, as well as on several other Internet directories. If you are unable to meet a farmer face-to-face, try visiting a locally owned food co-op or health food store. Often these shop managers will inspect each farm before agreeing to carry its grassfed and pastured products in their stores. Grassfed meats are increasingly available online, either from farms that ship their meats directly, or through grassfed meat purveyors that market cuts exclusively from farms that they've inspected. If you choose to use one of these online sources, take the time to call them first, asking them to explain their production or selection standards, making sure they're providing the quality you expect.

**On to the Grill**

There really is no better way to celebrate the warmth of summer, or take a reprieve from the doldrums of winter, than to step outside for some top-quality grilling and barbecue. Grassfed meat fares beautifully when cooked outdoors. The distinctive meat flavors—the beefier beef, nuttier pork, sweeter lamb and savory poultry—all taste magnificent when paired with a little flame and smoke. Animals raised on grass should result in a more variable product (see *The Beauty in Diversity*, p. 19), and grilling and barbecuing grassfed meats requires that you adopt a few new habits. All the recipes in this book have been written for and tested on grassfed beef and lamb, and pastured pork and poultry. But if you miss your old favorite standbys, with the following tenets, you can easily adapt any recipe to work with these meats.

1. *Get a thermometer...and then another one, and then another one*
2. *Tame your flame*
3. *Learn the difference between grilling, indirect grilling, and barbecue*

*4. Plan ahead*

*5. Throw out that store-bought BBQ sauce*

*1. Get a thermometer...and then another one, and then another one*

If you are familiar with my book *The Grassfed Gourmet*, you already know the importance of using a meat thermometer when cooking grassfed meat. While it is possible to roughly guess how long a certain cut of meat of a certain size will need to cook at a certain temperature, there is too much variability to know for sure.

Grass-based farms are not industrial factories. The livestock on these farms are unique individuals and their genetics are going to vary, which means that some animals will be fatter, some larger, some leaner, some older, and some younger when they are ready for processing. The types of grasses these animals eat will also vary. Occasionally, uninformed food critics complain that product variability is a problem in the grassfed meat industry. In my opinion, this variability is a healthy phenomenon (see *The Beauty in Diversity*, p. 19). The only problem occurs when cooks don't understand how to work with natural product variation.

Variation is not limited to the meat you buy. Grilling and barbecue are inexact sciences. You cannot simply turn a dial to a desired cooking temperature as you would on an oven, walk away, then return to perfectly cooked meat. You may learn that one chimney-full of coals or setting your grill dial to medium will yield a medium-hot flame, but this will not be true on a crisp fall day, or on a windy late-spring afternoon, or on somebody else's grill.

That's why we need to rely on thermometers. I'm a big fan of the digital instant-read thermometers available in most kitchen stores. These gadgets have a separate probe that is inserted in the meat and left there for the entire cooking process. This is a nice attribute, because you need puncture the meat only once, which minimizes the loss of juices. However, I have found that these probes do burn out with some frequency. If you choose to use this device, you might consider purchasing a few extra probes to keep on hand.

If you cannot afford a digital thermometer, or if your probe burns out and you don't have a replacement on hand, just keep a small, dial-faced food thermometer in your kitchen drawer. These are available in any hardware or kitchen store, and cost around five dollars. I do not like to rely on them too often because they require that you open the cooker and puncture the meat each time you check the temperature, but they are handy if you're on a budget, or as a back-up. They are also handy when working with a rotisserie, as the wires of the instant-read probe twist and tangle while the meat turns.

But when grill-roasting and barbecuing, you'll need more than just an internal meat thermometer. Until you are absolutely confident in your techniques, you'll also need to know the temperature of your grill when the lid is in place. Successful roasting of grass-fed meat outdoors requires that you carefully monitor the grill temperature to make sure it doesn't get too hot. This can be done with a grill thermometer. They are occasionally included on the outside of gas grills, but I don't often see them with charcoal setups. In that case, grill thermometers are also available at kitchen and hardware stores. In a pinch, you can use an oven thermometer. This is not a preferred option, however, since in order to read it, you must lift the grill lid, thereby letting out the heat you've built up. My newest gadget is the Maverick RediChek Remote Smoker Thermometer (available for about fifty dollars), which can monitor the grill and the meat temperature simultaneously. The wireless receiver lets me work around the house and chase after my daughter without having to constantly monitor the grill temp. It sounds an alarm if my fire gets too cool or too hot while barbecuing, so I know when to go out and adjust the vents or the coals.

### 2. Tame your flame

Gone are the days of barbarian appeal, when brave men built soaring fires, hurled the meat across the grate, then removed it when the crust was as black as the charcoal that fueled the fire, and the center was as gray as the ashes. Grassfed meat should be eaten rare to medium rare. The USDA has conditioned us to overcook our meat, claiming that internal temperatures lower than medium rare are considered unsafe. Since the agency assumes the use of meat from confinement feeding operations (feedlots) and industrialized meat packing facilities, it might not be bad advice. However, when it comes to grassfed meat from a trustworthy and known source, my personal practice is to cook to a considerably lower

# THE BEAUTY IN DIVERSITY

OK, I have a gripe. I have attended too many foodie and farm events where chefs and food critics have reprimanded pasture-based farmers, accusing them of producing "wildly inconsistent" products. Undoubtedly, the *quality* of meat is a critical factor. But *quality* is not synonymous with *consistency*...unless we're talking about consistently high quality.

*Consistency*, that is, *homogeneity*, is a value of the industrially based food system. When chefs get large quantities of meat off a delivery truck and plan to prepare 300 chicken breasts and 285 rib steaks for an enormous dinner, they expect that each chicken breast and each rib steak will be identical in taste, look, and preparation. They have been trained to expect this from our industrial food system, which specializes in factory-raised meat that, while not necessarily healthful or flavorful is, if nothing else, *consistent*. But reliance on this standardization can be a crutch to bypass true knowledge about food. Cooks need only follow the instructions they are given for cooking time and oven temperature, and need not be bothered with the nuances of variability, which require a more thorough understanding of the meat.

But the demand for consistency comes at a cost—not only to the true quality of the meat, but also to the environment, to the animals and to ourselves. To achieve uniformity, factory-farmed animals are fed unnatural rations of grain and artificial supplements, dosed with growth hormones and antibiotics, and stocked and processed in atrociously high concentration. The result is stressed and sickened animals, devastated and polluted landscapes, and meat that, to the enlightened palate, is flaccid, flavorless and, well, unnatural. But, hey, it's consistent—every piece just as lousy as the last!

Grassfed and pastured animals, by contrast, are responsive to the natural conditions in which they are raised. Animals harvested in the spring taste different than those harvested in the fall. The diversity of grasses on which the livestock graze impacts the flavor of the meat. The various animal breeds, which are generally chosen for their ability to thrive by grazing on pasture, have distinctive flavor and marbling qualities.

If grass-based farmers (or graziers) were to capitulate to standardization, we could only harvest in a limited season, which would disrupt the skillfully managed rotation of our pastures. We'd have to mechanically supplant our native pastures with a monoculture of selected grass species. If we all raised the same breed, we would risk losing forever the scores of different breeds and the genetics that have been carefully selected by generations of farmers. In short, we would again be trying to change the natural environment to suit our demands, rather than cultivating the very best of what Nature has to offer us.

The results of caving to this pressure would be a return to industrial agriculture: livestock that cannot thrive, reproduce, or even survive outside of a temperature-controlled environment, and the loss of the breeds that can; reduced biodiversity of our pastures, hedgerows and woodedge; and the susceptibility of livestock and monoculture pastures to disease or fluctuations in the weather.

But back to the matter of delicious, sublime meats...Grassfed meats are the culmination of the grass, clover and forbes species that flourished in a given year, the animal's genetic ancestry, the region where it was grown, the spirit of the farmer as he or she stewards the herds and land, and the unique attributes of the animal itself. When we consider fine wines, brewery beers or cheeses, such "inconsistencies" are not only accepted, but *prized* attributes, and so it should be with grassfed and pastured meats. As we explore and celebrate this regional variation, what the French call the *terroir*, we need only to learn the principles of cooking—using lower flames, monitoring internal temperatures, and understanding which cuts are most suitable for which methods. By using the principles of cooking grassfed meat, rather than adhering to a regimen of timetables and uniform instructions, we enable ourselves to successfully work with the inevitable—and wonderful—diversity inherent in sustainably raised meat.

internal temperature. Since grassfed meat can be leaner or less marbled than its conventional counterpart, it is likely to dry out and get chewy very quickly if cooked too hot and too fast.

That's not the only reason why you should consider enjoying your meat while it is still pink. Charred meats cooked fast, hot and well-done have been shown to contain two suspected carcinogens, Polycyclic Aromatic Hydrocarbons (PAHs) and heterocyclic amines (HCAs) (7). Ideally, to avoid these potential hazards, meat should be cooked at low temperatures and it should not be well-done—a happy coincidence, since this is the way that grassfed meat tastes best.

Many people habitually cook meat to well-done, fearing *E. coli*, a potentially harmful, even deadly, bacteria. But evidence has indicated that this hazard is greatly reduced in grassfed meats. In fact, *Science* magazine published a 1998 study that reported an *E. coli* count of 6,300,000 cells per gram of meat in grain-fed animals, as opposed to 20,000 cells per gram in grass-fed (8). Ordinarily, the *E. coli* bacteria found in grassfed meat is unlikely to survive our own digestive acids. However, a more virulent strain, *E. coli* O157:H7, has evolved in conventionally raised beef cows whose stomachs have become unnaturally acidic, owing to the grain-based diet fed in confinement farm operations. This potent form is more acid-resistant, and therefore can survive human stomach acids that would ordinarily have killed the less virulent strains. In grassfed cattle, not only is *E. coli* found in much lower numbers, it is still susceptible to our bodies' natural defenses (3).

Ultimately, how rare you eat your meat is a personal choice. When preparing grassfed meat, I advocate for internal temperatures far lower than the USDA recommendations. I believe the end result is better tasting and healthier for you. The chart below contains two different internal temperature ranges: one lists USDA recommendations, and the other shows my own preferences. If the internal temperatures I suggest are too low for you, feel free to use the USDA temperatures...just don't invite me to dinner!

| Meat | Suggested Internal Temperatures for Grassfed and Pastured Meats | USDA Recommended Internal Temperatures |
|---|---|---|
| Beef, Bison | 120–140° F | 145–170° F |
| Ground Meat | 160° F | 160° F |
| Veal | 125–155° F | 145–170° F |
| Lamb and Goat | 120–145° F | 145–170° F |
| Pork | 145–160° F | 160-170º F |
| Chicken (unstuffed) | 165° F | 165° F |
| Turkey (unstuffed) | 165° F | 165° F |

*3. Learn the difference between grilling, indirect grilling, spit-roasting and barbecue.*

There are four primary methods for cooking outdoors and, depending on the cut of meat you're preparing, each has its place.

**Grilling.** Grilling is what happens when you create a hot fire and place a cut of meat directly over it to cook. The typical cooking temperature can be in excess of 500 degrees F. A popular method for cooking conventional, grain-fed steaks, it should be rarely used when cooking grassfed meat. As a general rule—with the exception of the burgers, lamb chops, and hanger, flank and skirt steaks—forget about direct grilling. The results of grilling grassfed meat at such temperatures can be disastrous: it is too easy to over-cook it; there will be a higher incidence of flare-ups; plus there is a higher risk of generating those loathsome carcinogens, PAHs and HCAs.

**Indirect Grilling.** With indirect grilling, the heat source is kept to one side of the grill surface. The meat is briefly seared directly over the flame, then moved away from the heat and allowed to come up to temperature on the side of the grill that is not lit. To generate flavorful smoke, pre-soaked wood chips can be added, or they can be left out to create a less complicated taste comparable to oven roasting. The temperature inside the cooking chamber is often between 350–450 degrees F, but can be cooler. I'm a big advocate of indirect grilling; steaks and chops are less likely to get dried out and over-done. It is also a good method for cooking roasts, such as leg of lamb, pork loins, and whole chickens, but I find spit-roasting to be even better in these cases.

**Spit-Roasting.** Spit-roasting must be one of the most underrated outdoor cooking methods in this country. During the summer months, people cruise their farmers' markets seeking steaks, chops, chicken parts and the occasional pork shoulder for some old-fashioned pulled pork, but many folks overlook all the other splendid cuts of meat that can be cooked outdoors on a spit, relegating these cuts to wintertime oven-roasting. This is a pity, because these are some of the best meats you can turn out on a grill—whole chickens come out with perfectly crisped skin and juicy meat, sirloin roasts are browned on the outside and pink in the centers, whole legs of lamb glisten as they turn and yield succulent feasts. For about $130,

---

### GAUGING GRILL TEMPS

Once the lid of your grill is closed for indirect cooking or barbecue, you can monitor the temperature of the cooking chamber with a grill or smoker thermometer, much like an oven thermometer. But many recipes need to start out by making use of that direct flame, which is harder to gauge. Gas grills have dials that read "low," "medium" and "high" to give you an idea of flame intensity but, just like oven thermostats, they aren't especially precise. Whether you're using a charcoal or gas grill, the easiest way to gauge flame intensity is by the hand test. Holding your hand five inches above the grill surface, count the number of seconds you can leave it there before you have to pull away. A cool flame will be 6–8 seconds; medium will be 5 seconds, and hot will be 2–3 seconds. But bear in mind: it's a hand test, not a macho test! Remove your hand long before you singe your skin!

---

most companies offer rotisserie attachments for their grills, greatly expanding the variety of meat you can cook. I cannot emphasize enough how wonderful these gadgets are, particularly for grassfed meats. Rotisseries keep the meat well away from the flame, allow it to baste in its juices, and enable a slow, controlled cook unlike any other outdoor method. Plus, if you want to do a cookout and own a rotisserie, you can prepare the far less expensive cuts, the whole roasts, rather than shelling out big bucks for more expensive grill cuts, like porterhouse steaks or loin chops. You'll likely find that a rotisserie attachment will quickly pay for itself, both in savings from buying less-expensive meats, and by fool-proofing your grilling, providing you with perfectly cooked meats every time you cook outdoors.

**Barbecue.** Yum. Real barbecue was *made* for grassfed and pastured meat. Southern barbecue was an entrenched tradition long before the Civil War, when pigs were allowed to forage through the pastures, woodlots and fields. Likewise, when the Texans were perfecting beef barbecue, and Kentuckians were first feasting on barbecued mutton, their cattle and sheep were still roaming on grass.

Barbecue is all about slow cooking with smoke. The heat source is indirect and cool, never rising above 250 degrees F. Barbecue is ideal for cooking meats like pork butts, briskets and ribs, as the

---

## CHILL YOUR GRILL

Let's face it, when it comes to lowering the grill temperature, gas grills couldn't make it any easier. Lower the dial, or turn off all but one of the burners. Still, these grills may not burn as low as you'd like, or they may not burn as hot as you need them to when searing your steaks.

Charcoal grills offer the benefit of a wider temperature range, but you need to know how to control it. Here are a few ways to cool down a too-hot charcoal grill:

• Close the vents on the top of the lid (the exhaust).
• Close the vents in the base of the kettle (the intake—often there is a lever or wheel on the bottom of the grill).
• Keep a mixing bowl of water near your grill. If the fire gets too hot, remove a few hot coals and toss them into the water. Alternatively, add a little wet charcoal or soaked smoking wood chips to the fire.
• Keep a spray bottle of water on hand, and spritz the embers to temper the heat.

---

slow moist heat breaks down tough connective tissues, called collagen, making these cuts juicy and tender. It is also the perfect method for cooking large roasts, like fresh hams, a side of beef or whole animals, such as an entire pig, a lamb or a turkey.

Authentic barbecue often uses "pits," Willy Wonka-esque cookers where the cool fire smolders in a firebox separate from the cooking chamber. But you don't have to buy an elaborate barbecue pit to enjoy good barbecue. Using a method similar to indirect grilling, a low fire can be maintained on one side of your charcoal kettle or gas grill, with the meat placed on the opposite side. Soaked wood chips such as hickory, apple or mesquite are placed on the fire to generate smoke. If using a charcoal grill, the lid is set so that the vents open above the meat, drawing the smoke across the grill and through the roast, giving it the same luscious flavor that comes from a barbecue pit.

### 4. Plan ahead

This is good advice whenever you're cooking, but it is especially important when you want to cook outdoors. I've ruined a lot of good food by failing to plan a meal until the last minute. Imagine the scene: It's after 7PM. We're just getting home from the farm. I have a cranky, hungry toddler on my hands, the dog is famished, bedtime is rapidly approaching, the kitchen is a disaster, and the grill isn't even warmed up. The idea of grilling at this point is annoying at best, but it's just too darn hot to start up the kitchen stove. And so, I trudge out to the grill in a hurry, get the flames searing hot, heave on the steaks and hope for the best. Meanwhile, I try to get my daughter to take her bath, my husband cleans up the kitchen and makes a salad, and the rib-eyes are turned into beef jerky. Dinner is ruined *and* late.

From personal experience I can vouch that, with a little advance prep, a complete gorgeous meal can be prepared in less than 30 minutes. I try to think about dinner long before it happens —ideally, one or two days ahead, but at least the morning before. Frozen meat can be taken out early so that it can thaw without having to use a microwave. Spice rubs or marinades can be prepared and applied to meat early in the day, allowing flavor to build while we work and our daughter naps and plays. I allow time to ready the grill for cooking (20 minutes for gas, 30 minutes for charcoal).

If I know I'm going to be busy during the week, I try to make large batches of side dishes—coleslaw, tomato and cucumber salads, cornbread—in advance, so they're on hand. If I'm planning to barbecue, I do it on the days when I work near the house, and make sure that I have plenty of grill fuel (charwood, or a full tank of propane) on hand. I start early and monitor the fire often. If all of these efforts fail (and yes, they occasionally do), go for the hamburgers and sausages (grassfed, of course).

Grilling and barbecue are not mystifying rituals to be practiced only by pit masters with lifelong training and membership in secret societies. They are easy and enjoyable ways to keep the heat out of your kitchen and create flavorful food, provided you take time to plan.

### 5. Throw out your bottle of store-bought barbecue sauce

Did you ever look at the ingredients list on that stuff? It's predominantly high fructose corn syrup. While classic barbecue requires that we add a little sweetness to the mixture, drowning everything from the grill with a bottle of flavored corn syrup does not result in great dining. This book contains a number of sauce recipes for exciting grilling and barbecue variations. If you don't have time to make them, consider purchasing "homemade" bottled sauces from your farmers' market or local specialty food store. They will likely contain much less sugar, probably no corn syrup, and have a much more authentic flavor.

Beyond that, one of the best ways to season grassfed meat is with herb and spice rubs, mild marinades and pastes. Unlike conventional meat, grassfed products have true flavor and texture. Overpowering super-sweet sauces mask the natural meat taste. Conversely, rubs and pastes will build the flavor profile, allowing you to savor your meat's natural richness and sweetness, as well as the fun seasonings that can accompany it.

### Choosing your Grill

There are countless grills available across the U.S. and Canada today—kettle charcoal barbecues, table grills, hibachis, elaborate professional-grade gas grill outdoor kitchens, built-in brick or tile grill-ovens, steel drums sawed in half and fitted with grates, Big

Green Eggs, hybrid gas-charcoal grills, barbecue pits, plus an enormous array of smokers. For the sake of keeping things straightforward and accessible, all the recipes in this book are written to work with simple gas grills and charcoal kettles. Once you learn the techniques, you can get as fancy as you want. Whichever grill you opt to work with is a matter of personal preference.

Some people prefer gas grills because they feel they are more convenient and effortless to light, they burn cleaner, and it is easier to control the flame. Those who prefer charcoal grills often like how they flavor the food, the more dynamic temperature control, their inexpensive cost, and the sensual pleasure of interacting directly with the mechanics of the heat. I like to think of it as the difference between people who drive cars with stick shifts, and people with automatics. I happen to be a charcoal user. All the reasons above apply, but for me the main reason is that I once singed my eyebrows while trying to light a malfunctioning gas grill. Thus, in my backyard, the low technology of charcoal has infinitely more appeal. Whichever you choose, here are the steps to get your flames ready for the food.

### Starting a gas grill
To start, refer to your owner's manual for lighting instructions. When lighting the grill, make sure the lid is open. Open the dial on the tank to allow the propane to flow, turn the starter burner on high,

---

## SUSTAINABLE GRILLING

According to the Sierra Club, Americans light an estimated 60 million grills each Fourth of July, consuming enough energy to power 20,000 households for a year. Tristan West, a research scientist with the U.S. Department of Energy, says that July Fourth grilling festivities alone release 225,000 metric tons of carbon dioxide into the air.

In an ideal world these emissions could be eliminated altogether if everyone exchanged their grills for solar ovens. But solar ovens, while capable of producing wonderful dishes, are suited to an entirely different style of cooking. Furthermore, those of us who regularly find ourselves barbecuing under clouds and rain would probably discover a whole new definition of "slow cooking" using solar technology. Most grills used in this country are either powered with charcoal or wood, or natural gas or propane. Natural gas and propane offer the environmental benefits of burning cleaner and more efficiently, but they are nonrenewable petroleum products. Charcoal and wood are more polluting, but offer the advantages of coming from trees, a renewable resource. Whichever barbecue technology you opt for, there are still ways to make the entire experience more earth-friendly.

Purchase a good quality grill. Not only will it cook more efficiently, but a good quality grill will last you many years, as opposed to a junk-store cheapie that will clutter up a landfill after only a season or two. Be sure to keep the grill covered and well-maintained to prevent rust and corrosion.

Stop using lighter fluid. Made from petroleum distillates, lighter fluid releases fumes into the air—volatile organic compounds (VOCs)—which contribute to ground-level ozone pollution. (Ground level ozone forms when nitrogen oxides and VOCs combine in warm air.) In addition to polluting your community, lighter fluid contributes to a number of ground-level ozone-related health problems and can leave potentially toxic chemical residues on your food. I recommend beautifully low-tech charcoal chimney starters. They are safer, cheaper over the long haul, easy to use, and better for the environment. If you have an electricity source near your grill, an electric charcoal starter will work, too.

Choose your charcoal wisely. The standard composition briquettes, which look like perfectly uniform little pillows and are available in most grocery stores, are not only bad for your health, they're not so great for the planet, either. While they contain wood fibers, they are mostly comprised of lumber mill scraps and sawdust, and therefore need coal dust and petroleum-based additives to act as binders. Especially suspect are the self-starting briquettes, which have been soaked in lighter fluid. There is such a thing as natural briquettes, made from pulverized lump charcoal that is then bonded with natural starches. I live in a very rural area and have not managed to locate this product near me.

I use lump charcoal, or "charwood." Lump charcoal from properly managed forests has a number of advantages over composition briquettes. It burns hotter, which means you can use, *at most*, half the normal amount to start your grill. I find myself using about one-third the ordinary amount that would be required for a briquette fire. (You will, however, need to add coals a little more often than you would with composition briquettes.) Charwood ignites more easily and promotes better flavor. It also greatly speeds up your grilling time. Where you need to budget 30 minutes to have a charcoal grill ready using briquettes, you'll only need 20 minutes with lump charcoal, making it more comparable to gas grilling. It is commonly offered for sale with most grilling supplies. I buy mine through our local hardware store and at our local health food store.

Real sustainably harvested hardwoods such as apple, hickory, oak or mesquite are also wonderful grill fuels that deliver intense heat, great flavor and long burning times. If you choose to use natural wood, allow the wood to burn to just embers before cooking. Resist the temptation to burn your scrap lumber or plywood, which release toxic chemicals. Also, avoid using softwood like pine, which releases a lot of resins as it burns.

and press the ignition button. If the grill doesn't light after you've pushed the ignition button a few times, turn *everything* off, leave the lid on the grill open, and allow the gas to dissipate for a minute or two before repeating the process. If you continue to push the ignition button without starting over, you'll have a miniature explosion, putting your eyebrows in jeopardy. Yes, I speak from experience.

Once the starter burner is lit, turn on the remaining burners, close the lid, and allow the grill to heat for 10 to 15 minutes, until it reaches your desired cooking temperature. Once the temperature has been achieved, turn off any unnecessary burners, scrape the grate clean with a wire bristle brush, and start cooking your supper. After you've finished cooking, be sure to clean the grate with the wire brush once more.

### Starting a charcoal grill

Ok, repeat after me: "I will never, *ever* use lighter fluid or gasoline to start my fire." Gasoline is just plain dangerous. And while lighter fluid might seem acceptable since it was created for that express purpose, it is also pretty nasty. Not only is it environmentally disastrous (see *Sustainable Grilling*, p. 26), lighter fluid contains a number of dangerous substances that can leave residues on your food. It also makes things taste like they were cooked on your car engine.

I think the easiest, most environmentally responsible way to start charcoal grills is by using a special chimney that is available in any store that sells barbecue supplies. A simple vented cylinder with a handle, these chimneys hold a pile of charcoal, charwood or wood chunks on top, and have a concave space at the bottom where you can insert crumpled up newspaper. Once you've filled the chimney, light the newspaper, then allow it to burn and ignite the coals. The coals are ready to be dumped into the grill when they are edged with a thin layer of gray ash, usually in about 10 minutes.

Always make sure you're using enough charcoal. It is easy (especially if you're frugal, like me) to skimp on the number of coals. Too often, the end result is a wimpy fire and improperly cooked food. As a gauge, when direct grilling, use enough charcoal to slightly exceed the space on the grill needed to cook your food. If, instead of briquettes, you're using lump charcoal (also called

In addition to a good grill, there are a few more things you might like to have on hand for enjoying a great grassfed cookout.

**Drip pan.** Handy for catching messy drippings when cooking fattier foods, preventing them from spattering on the fire. I'm especially fond of using a drip pan when barbecuing and indirect grilling meats like chicken or pork roasts, where I want to preserve as much juice as possible for swabbing my meat morsels after. Alternatively (or additionally), consider a cast-iron pan (see below).

**Rotisserie**. Most good quality grills have rotisserie attachments available for them. If you can spare the extra $130, I think it is a worthwhile investment when working with grassfed meat. In fact, I insist that you buy one, since I've written several recipes which require it! While they seem to have fallen out of fashion in the States, they remain popular in countries that still cook a lot of grassfed and pastured meats. Rotisseries help keep the meat out of the flames, ensuring a slow, even cook, particularly helpful when working with leaner cuts of beef and lamb. At the same time, they provide a nice even sear on the outside, creating a delicious crust. Better still, because they are constantly revolving, your roasts, ribs, and chickens baste in their own juices. Your instant-read thermometer will not be very useful in this case, since the wires on the probe are likely to get tangled with the rotations. Thus, you'll have to rely more heavily on the time gauges I've provided in the book, stopping the rotisserie periodically towards the end of the cooking time to verify with your thermometer.

**Skewers.** Most farmers I know offer gorgeous lamb, beef and pork kebabs, some of the best grilling goodies you'll ever find. Too often, I've seen customers pine after them at farmers' markets, imagining the luscious marinades they'll use to prepare them for dinner that night...only to suddenly remember that they have no skewers. Bamboo skewers are usually available in grocery stores, but nothing beats the convenience of durable metal skewers stored in your kitchen drawer, able to handle weights that would snap most bamboo, and ready for kebabs in the blink of an eye without requiring any soaking time first.

**Cast-iron cookware.** Made for cooking directly in the fire, cast iron is a grassfed cook's dream-come-true. When working with leaner roasts, I like to put the meat in a cast-iron pan to capture the juices. It is infinitely friendlier on the environment than a disposable aluminum pan, more effective than a drip pan, and easy to clean up. Grill-roasting or barbecuing imparts wonderful flavor to cast iron, and the smoke only adds to the pan's seasoning. When you bring your pan back indoors, the foods you cook on your stove will taste even better.

charwood)—and for the purposes of this book I will assume you are (see *Sustainable Grilling*, p. 26)—you can get away with using considerably less.

When the coals are ready, dump them onto the bottom grate and use tongs to arrange them as specified in the recipe. Most of the recipes in this book use barbecue or indirect grilling techniques.

For these, either pile all the coals on one side, or arrange them around the perimeter of the grill, leaving a fire-free zone to cook your food after it has been seared. I usually find it easiest to pile them all to one side, especially when searing.

After you've arranged the coals, set the cooking grate in place, put the lid on, and allow the entire grill to heat up for five minutes. Once the grate is good and hot, clean it with a wire brush. If oiling the grate will be necessary, do so just before adding the food. After you've finished cooking, brush the grill with the wire brush once more.

In this book you'll find chapters devoted exclusively to beef, lamb, pork and poultry. All of these recipes have been tested on grassfed meats, using the grilling and barbecue techniques outlined above. I've noted which ones are most kid-friendly, which work best on a budget, which require minimal preparation, and which ones work well for an elegant feast or for serving company.

As you read through this book, consider the positive impact you are making by choosing a trusted source of grassfed, sustainably grown and harvested meats. As you sit down with your family and friends to enjoy a great meal, know that through the celebration of fabulous food, we are also honoring the planet and the bounty of our farming communities.

I wish you a magnificent and delicious journey!

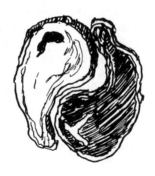

1. K. Clancy, "Greener Pastures: How grass-fed beef and milk contribute to healthy eating," Union of Concerned Scientists, March 2006.

2. F. Diez-Gonzalez, et al., "Grain-feeding and the Dissemination of Acid-resistant Escherichia Coli from Cattle," *Science* 281 (1998): 1666.

3. J.B. Russell, F. Diez-Gonzalez, and G. N. Jarvis, "Potential Effect of Cattle Diets on the Transmission of Pathogenic Escherichi Coli to Humans," *Microbes Infect* 2, no.1 (2000): 45–53.

4. S. Durham, "From Dirt to Diamonds," United States Department of Agriculture Agricultural Research Service, July 29, 2005.

5. L. Burras and J. McLaughlin, "Soil Organic Carbon in fields of switch grass and row crops as well as woodlots and pastures across the Chariton Valley, Iowa," Iowa State University, 2002.

6. J. Robinson, "The Brand Name Bandwagon," Eatwild.com, 2003.

7. P. Lavelle, "Throw another tumour on the Barbie," Australian Broadcasting Corporation, February 10, 2005.

8. S. Stevens, "Hearth & Home: P's and Q's of BBQ. A guide to guilt-free grilling," *Sierra Magazine*, July/August 2005.

CHAPTER TWO

# Beef

Beef, brazenly seared over tempestuous flames, then patiently coaxed up to temperature indirectly in the fire's aura, forms a savory crust reminiscent of caramel, chicory and all things sensed not in the nose, but deep in the chest, close to the heart, like robust laughter, a child's hug, or simmering passion. In nearly every country, where there is a grill, there is beef.

At our weekly farmers' market, the visitors drift by and we come to know their faces well—there are our regular customers, the meat-eaters, and then there are the "recovering vegetarians." We always smile when a committed vegetarian market-goer tells us she is pregnant—often, before the second trimester is over, she is standing in front of our market stall, suddenly eager for ground beef, rib-eye steaks, short ribs, anything that she can persuade her husband to toss on the fire for her. She wants clean meat from a reliable source, and it's exciting to see her become attuned with her own nutritional needs.

Beef nourishes us deeply. It is rich in easily digestible macro and trace minerals, an excellent source of B-12, and contains fat-soluble vitamins and essential fatty acids. And when the meat comes from grassfed animals, the taste is incomparable. The flavors of the minerals come through in a grassfed steak, the palate feels clean, and the textures are more pronounced, not flaccid and mushy, as with factory-farmed steaks.

Grass farmers all across the country are making huge strides in perfecting the overall quality of pasture-raised beef. By wise tending of pasture health and livestock genetics, skillful animal husbandry, and careful monitoring of processing and butchering, a lot of grassfed beef now grades "choice," or occasionally even "prime," resulting in rich, savory meat bursting with juice and flavor. As the grassfed meat movement has developed into a true artisan craft, it is possible to produce meat that is handsomely marbled and tender without relying on corn and other supplements.

That said, the grilling techniques I've described in the following pages are designed to work with lean meat. I feel these are the best techniques for several reasons. First, while a lot of grassfed beef grades choice, meaning it is well-marbled, some does not.

---

## GRAIN FINISHING

Contrary to industrial convention, the artisan grazier knows that it is completely unnecessary to fatten, or "finish," grassfed beef on grain. Some nutritional experts keen on increasing the fat content of the meat have argued that finishing ruminants on grain simply replicates a wild animal's ability to forage a fall harvest of wild grains and nuts. It is true that beef fat is extremely nutritious, but fattening on grain just prior to harvest does not replicate any natural phenomenon. A grazing animal in the wild would find only a relatively small amount of such high-calorie foods, as the mainstay diet is grasses and other leafy forage. Grain fed at the trough stresses and acidifies the animal's digestive system, which is uniquely designed to digest grasses. (This elevated stomach acidity is also implicated in the appearance of the super-virulent strain of *E. coli*, O157:H7.)

Moreover, the production, harvest, transport and feeding of grain, even organic grain, to ruminants, is a shamefully inefficient use of our resources. In most climates the amount of acreage required to produce grain for cattle is significantly greater than the land that would be required to sustain them on grass. Furthermore, producing the amount of grain required by industrial feedlots demands massive use of fossil fuels, irrigation, and, in most cases, chemical treatment. Whereas before, the norm was to allow grazing animals to walk to plants to feed, modern industrial convention is now in the perverse situation of transporting plants to animals who are forced to stand in place!

Truthfully, most consumers have a difficult time discerning the difference between choice and select-grade meat (the next highest marbling grade, which most grassfed beef easily attains). Grassfed meat is the product of an artisanal, ecologically diverse food system, which means that variability is natural. Farmers cultivate a variety of genetics to secure the vigor of their herds, different seasons (and regions) offer different pasture, and some grazing seasons are more bountiful than others. Such factors mean that two beef, even if raised side by side, may present subtle differences in flavor and marbling. Sustainably grown food will have natural variation.

The trick in dealing with variability in meat is in its handling. Using these grilling and barbecue techniques, a lean steak will be every bit as delicious as a well-marbled one. Furthermore, these techniques are healthier for you.

When grilling meats such as steaks, resist bringing the meat near the fire before the flame is adequately hot (for each recipe, I've given instructions on gauging adequate fire heat). When the coals are ready, sear the cuts for only a few minutes directly over the fire, then promptly move the meat off the coals to the unlit portion of the grill, where it will come up to temperature "in the fire's aura." This technique minimizes contact with carcinogenic hydrocarbons associated with cooking over open flames, while still creating that great savory sear that epitomizes the quintessential steak. Also, by patiently allowing the meat to come up to temperature slowly, you are less likely to over-cook your steaks.

For *asado*-style cooking—a technique for grilling short ribs (among other cuts)—the meat is allowed to sit directly over coals for two hours or more, using heat transfer through the bone to cook the meat, not the flame itself. The short ribs are placed bone-side down so that the fleshy part does not come in contact with the flame except at the very end for a brief sear. When using a traditional Argentine *parilla*, or open grill pit, the *asador* keeps a fire burning to one side and shovels glowing embers under the grill, allowing the meat to slowly cook over intense heat, but with no flames. However, the great Argentinean flavor can also be captured using a rotisserie on an American grill. If you are inclined to construct your own *parilla*, see chapter 6, where the classic *parilla* methods are discussed.

For slow-smoking, the cooking chamber of your grill will be kept cool, creating an effect similar to a slow braise, reducing the likelihood that the proteins of the meat will be denatured. Because the meat is cooked at such low temperatures, tough cuts will be made tender, much like a pot roast. This process may take more time than you have to tend to the grill, so don't be ashamed of smoking your chuck steaks or briskets for a few hours, then finishing them in a covered roasting pan in a moderate oven with a little barbecue sauce. The meat can even be refrigerated after smoking, then finished in an oven at a more convenient time. This is a great technique to use when you have a few spare hours to tend to a grill on the weekend, but then want to enjoy great barbecue pit flavor on a busy weeknight.

# THE BEST STEAK

In my grassfed grilling workshops, we work with three seasonings: salt, pepper and garlic. When you are working with flavorful meat, there is very little seasoning required. What matters is how you handle the fire and the meat. Whether you're cooking filet mignon, top loin, rib-eye, top blade, T-bone or porterhouse steaks, the basic method is the same.

> *Elegant*
> *Minimal preparation*
> *On a budget (depending on which steak you*
> *choose, see* **Choosing A Steak,** *p. 37)*
> *Serves 2 (If steaks are boneless, allow 1/2 pound*
> *per person. For bone-in steaks, allow 1 pound*
> *per person.)*

> **1–2 tablespoons coarse salt**
> **2–3 teaspoons ground black pepper**
> **2 gloves garlic, minced**
> **Either 1 sirloin, sirloin tip, tri-tip, top round or**
> **London broil steak; OR 2 shoulder top blade,**
> **shoulder petite tender, rib, porterhouse, T-**
> **bone, top loin (NY strip), or tenderloin (filet**
> **mignon) steaks. Steaks should be about 1 1/2**
> **inches thick.**

Combine the salt, pepper and garlic in a small bowl. Rub the mixture into both sides of the steak, then allow the meat to come to room temperature while you prepare the grill.

Start the grill and warm it until it is medium-hot. If you are using a gas grill, turn off all but one of the burners once it has come up to temperature. If you are using charcoal, be sure all the coals have been raked to one side. Using the hand test, the grate will be hot enough when you can hold your palm five inches above the metal for no more than three seconds.

Sear the steaks for 3 minutes on each side directly over the flame, with the lid down. Then, move steaks to the part of the grill that is not lit. Set the lid in place and allow the steaks to cook, without flipping them, until they reach 120–140 degrees F , about 15–25 minutes, depending on the size of the steak. Remove the steaks to a platter and tent loosely with foil, allowing steaks to rest 5 minutes before serving (the temperature will come up a few more degrees during this time).

## CHOOSING A STEAK

My husband and I don't like to think of ourselves simply as *meat vendors* at our farmers' market. Rather, we prefer to regard ourselves as *dinner consultants*. Our job is not to sell the most expensive cut of meat to our customers. Instead, our true calling on Saturday market days is to pair customers with the *right* cut of meat.

This is especially true when people approach us with a hankering for a good steak. Steaks come in numerous shapes and sizes, and can be selected to accommodate all budgets, but most people don't understand the differences among them. Customers have a tendency to reach for the steak with the most familiar name, without knowing that there might be a better match for their palate and pocketbook. We seldom let any new customer buy a cut of beef for their grill without a thorough consultation—or a little nosey intervention. It's our way of guaranteeing there are no mis-*steaks* (ha). Here are some notes on the different steaks out there, in hopes that you'll be able to make the best selection for you and your dinner companions. As best as possible, I've listed them according to price, the most expensive cuts appearing first. Please note, however, that pricing structures vary from farm to farm.

*Tenderloin Steak*: Also called filet mignon, *fillet de boeuf,* fillet steak, or,

when left whole, châteaubriand. This is the most expensive cut of meat on the beef. It comes from the short loin, the strip of muscle that does the least amount of work when the animal moves around. There is only a little bit to be had per animal (tenderloin only makes up about 2% of the meat on a beef carcass), and this boneless cut is extremely tender, although not as richly flavored as meat coming from more active parts of the animal.

*Porterhouse:* These bone-in steaks come from the short loin and contain a piece of the tenderloin. Because they contain bone (which adds some flavor) and only a strip of the short loin, they are less expensive than a tenderloin steak, although they are still quite pricey. However, on occasion, they can be a financially prudent choice if two people want a premium steak and are willing to share. The porterhouse is usually big enough for two portions.

*T-Bone:* Also cut from the short loin, T-bones look very similar to porterhouses, only with a much smaller piece of tenderloin attached. They usually cost less per pound, have the bone for flavor, but typically only serve one person.

*Top Loin:* Also called strip steak, boneless club steak, hotel-style steak, Kansas City steak, New York strip steak. This is a piece of the short loin with no tenderloin attached. It may or may not be boneless. If you prefer leaner cuts of meat with a good amount of tenderness thrown in, this is a good choice. While these are more expensive than some of the steaks that follow, they can be a good buy because there is very little waste (like grizzle and bone) left on the plate.

*Rib Eye and Rib Steaks:* Also called Delmonico, market or Spencer steaks. Cut from the rib, these steaks are typically well-marbled and juicy. They may or may not have a bone. Those rib eyes cut closer to the chuck will be larger and more likely to serve two to three people; those cut from farther back are smaller, often more tender, and are more appropriate as single servings.

*Sirloin Steak:* This juicy, moderately tender steak from the sirloin is somewhat lean and has very little waste. Typically large and boneless, it is an excellent steak for feeding multiple people. Figure on 1/2 pound per person when selecting the appropriate piece.

*Tri-tip Steak:* (Can also be cut as a sirloin tip steak.) Slightly chewier than the sirloin (although with good grassfed beef, the difference will be *very* hard to discern), this cut has a tad more flavor, but otherwise is very similar to the sirloin steak.

*London Broil:* This is a confusing name, because the London was once exclusively cut from the flank, but now comes from either the sirloin or the top round. Leaner and chewier, these steaks hold up especially well to marinades. They are a good budget choice and offer the creative cook lots of possibilities.

*Flank Steak:* Cut from the flank and characterized by its evident longitudinal grain, the flank steak in this country is typically thin-cut and chewy. It is prized by Tex-Mex aficionados, as well as anyone who loves great beefy flavor.

*Skirt Steak:* Cut from the plate of the beef and typically priced similarly to the flank, this quick-cooking steak is often used interchangeably with the flank.

*Top Blade Steak:* Also called flatiron, book steak, blade steak, lifter steak or Butler steak, this is one of the great unknown gems of the steak world. Cut from the chuck, top blade steaks are well-kept secrets; chewier than a top loin, but more tender than a flank or skirt, they have all the robust flavor of the chuck. It is a moderately tender and very tasty choice, and can easily be substituted for flanks or skirts, or cooked like a top loin.

*Mock Tender:* Also called petite tender, these cuts look identical to tenderloin steaks, but they come from the chuck. In fact, some unscrupulous grocery stores have been known to mislead their shoppers, pawning these off as filet mignon. Provided you are not charged filet prices, these are wonderful little morsels of meat to stumble upon. Naturally chewier than cuts from the short loin, they are nonetheless quite tender, full of flavor, and easy on the budget.

*Chuck Steak:* Cut from the chuck, the first slices are taken right next to the rib-eye and are therefore nearly as tender at a fraction of the cost. These cuts can be grilled without trouble. Cuts taken farther on from the rib will progressively get larger and chewier, but lend themselves well to smoking. Chucks are prized for their marbling and superior taste. They are preferred steaks by those of us who hang out in the butcher's quarters, who prize rich flavor above all else.

# Grilled Steaks
# in a Cilantro-Olive Paste

These seasonings sound showy but, in truth, they perform as subtle accents, highlighting the full-beef flavor of the steaks. And while they are perfectly elegant fare, my toddler daughter loves to gnaw on the bones and taste the black olives in the seasoning.

*Elegant*
*Kid-friendly*
*Minimal preparation*
*On a budget (depending on which steak you*
    *choose)*
*Serves 2-4 (If steaks are boneless, allow 1/2 pound*
    *per person. For bone-in steaks, allow 1 pound*
    *per person.)*

**1/2 cup fresh cilantro**
**3 ounces pitted black olives**
**1 teaspoon coarse salt**
**1/2 teaspoon freshly ground black pepper**
**2 tablespoons olive oil**
**1 clove garlic**
**Either 1 sirloin, sirloin tip, tri-tip, top round or**
    **London broil steak; OR 2 shoulder top blade,**
    **shoulder petite tender, rib, porterhouse, T-**
    **bone, top loin (NY strip), tenderloin (filet**
    **mignon) steaks. The steak you choose should**
    **be about 1 1/2 inches thick.**

Add the first six ingredients to a food processor and purée, making a paste. Generously coat the steaks and allow them to come to room temperature.

Start the grill and warm it until it is medium-hot. If you are using a gas grill, turn off all but one of the burners once it has come up to temperature. If you are using charcoal, be sure all the coals have been raked to one side. Using the hand test, the grate will be hot enough when you can hold your palm five inches above it for no more than three seconds.

Sear the steaks for 3 minutes on each side directly over the flame, with the lid down. Then, move steaks to the part of the grill that is not lit. Set the lid in place and allow the steaks to cook, without flipping them, until they reach 120-140 degrees F, about 15-25 minutes, depending on the size of the steak. Remove the steaks to a platter and tent loosely with foil, allowing steaks to rest five minutes before serving (the temperature will come up a few more degrees during this time).

## FOR THE FREESTYLE HOT-SHOT GRILLERS

All right. You have a crowd for dinner and you want to dazzle them with your intuitive grilling prowess. It's only natural that you might be a little furtive about testing the doneness of their steaks with an internal meat thermometer (which, if no one's looking, you can do by inserting the probe into the side of the steak). Personally, I think there's nothing to be ashamed of, particularly since you'll be able to present your guests with perfectly grilled steaks. Still, we all like to look hip at the flames now and then, so if you want to leave your thermometer in the kitchen drawer, use the firmness-to-touch method for gauging doneness.

*However*—make sure you practice a few times with the meat thermometer for verification before you show off with this trick!!

First, find the fleshy part of your hand between your thumb and index finger. Let your hand hang limp, then press this spot. If this is how the steak feels, then the meat is rare. Next, stretch out your fingers, but allow your thumb to hang down. The fleshy part will now feel like a medium-rare steak. Finally, close your hand to a fist and touch the spot once more. This is how a well-done steak will feel.

Rare

Medium

Well-done

# Sirloin Tip Marinated in Tamarind and Apple Butter

Sirloin tip steaks, as their name suggests, come from the end of the sirloin. They are not as tender as sirloin steaks and, like London broils, work beautifully with marinades. This is a wonderful steak to use if you are serving guests and don't have a lot of money to spend. There is very little waste with a sirloin tip, and often 1 steak can serve 3-4 people. Be sure to cut it across the grain, just as you would a London broil, to enjoy maximum tenderness. One note—if you don't have a lot of time to marinate the meat, this recipe also tastes great if you apply the marinade as a seasoning paste and then cook it immediately.

Tamarind paste, a seasoning used often in Indian cooking, can be found in most specialty food and large grocery stores. For a substitute paste, see p. 117.

*Good for company*
*Minimal preparation*
*On a budget*
*Serves 3-4*

1 teaspoon tamarind paste
2 tablespoons apple butter
2 tablespoons freshly grated ginger
1/4 cup olive oil
2 cloves crushed garlic
2 teaspoons salt
3 tablespoons cider vinegar
1/2 teaspoon cayenne pepper
1/2 small onion, finely chopped
1 sirloin tip steak or London broil, 1 1/2–2 pounds

Whisk together the first 9 ingredients, then pour into a baking pan or plastic zip-lock bag. Add the steak and thoroughly coat it with the marinade, cover, refrigerate, and allow it to marinate several hours or overnight. Before cooking, remove it from the refrigerator, blot the steak dry, and allow it to come to room temperature before you start your grill.

Start the grill and warm it until it is medium-hot. If you are using a gas grill, turn off all but one of the burners once it has come up to temperature. If you are using charcoal, be sure all the coals have been raked to one side. Using the hand test, the grate will be hot enough when you can hold your palm five inches above it for no more than three seconds.

Sear the steaks for 3 minutes on each side directly over the flame, then move them to the part of the grill that is not lit. Set the lid in place and allow the steaks to cook, without flipping them, until they reach 120–140 degrees F, about 20–30 minutes. Remove the meat to a platter and tent loosely with foil, allowing the meat to rest five minutes before serving (the temperature will come up a few more degrees during this time).

# BLACK PEPPER BURGERS

I've experimented with a lot of burger recipes, but this simple version remains my favorite. This recipe is easy and flavorful, and the generous spread of black pepper on the surface gives it a fun, spicy and crispy outer texture while still allowing the grassfed beef taste to shine through.

*Tip:* If you find that your burgers don't hold together well, try adding a tablespoon of breadcrumbs to the mixture before forming the patties.

*Kid-friendly*
*On a budget*
*Minimal preparation*
*Serves 4*

**2 tablespoons salt**
**2 tablespoons whole black peppercorns, coarsely crushed**
**1 1/2 pounds ground beef, ideally 80% lean**

Combine the salt and meat in a shallow bowl. Loosely shape the ground beef into approximately four meatballs. Roll the balls in the pepper until they are lightly coated, then gently flatten them until they are just shy of being one-inch thick. With your fingertips, make a small well in the top of each patty to prevent the meat from getting puffy over the flames. Set the patties aside while you light the grill and clean off the cooking grate with a wire brush.

When the grill is medium-hot and you can hold your hand five inches above it for no more than three or four seconds, brush the grill down lightly with vegetable oil, then set the patties directly over the flame, with the well facing up. Grill, covered, for about 4 minutes per side for medium burgers, remembering that, for safety, ground beef should be cooked to a minimum internal temperature of 160 degrees.

# MUSHROOM AND OLIVE BURGERS

No matter how timid you are in the kitchen, you should always experiment with new burger recipes. I've tried them with salsa, grated cheese, chilis—whatever ingredients I had on hand. My all-time favorite add-in, however, is olives. In this black olive version, the mushrooms add a nice earthy note that pairs well with the beef. As I mentioned earlier, if you are having trouble getting your patties to hold together, try adding a tablespoon of breadcrumbs to the recipe.

*Good for company*
*Kid-friendly*
*Minimal preparation*
*On a budget*
*Serves 4*

1/4 cup fresh chives, finely chopped
1/4 cup fresh mushrooms, diced
1/4 cup oil-cured black olives, pitted and finely
    chopped
3 tablespoons fresh oregano, finely chopped, or 1
    tablespoon dried
1 1/2 teaspoons coarse salt
2 teaspoons coarsely ground black pepper
1 clove garlic, minced
1 1/2 pounds ground beef, ideally 80% lean

Combine the chives, mushrooms, olives, oregano, salt, pepper and garlic in a medium-sized bowl. Mix well. Add the ground beef. Using your hands, mix until all the ingredients are thoroughly incorporated into the meat. Loosely shape the beef into 4 meatballs, then gently flatten each ball until it is just shy of one-inch thick. With your fingertips, make a small well in the top of each patty to prevent the meat from getting puffy over the flames. Set the patties aside while you light the grill and brush off the cooking grate.

When the grill is medium-hot and you can hold your hand five inches above it for no more than three or four seconds, brush it down lightly with vegetable oil, then set the patties directly over the flame, with the well facing up. Grill, covered, for about 4–5 minutes per side for medium burgers, remembering that, for safety, ground beef should be cooked to a minimum internal temperature of 160 degrees.

---

### NEW TO GRASSFED? THEN YOUR FIRST STEAK OFF THE GRILL SHOULD BE...A HAMBURGER!

Yes, I mean it. A hamburger. I encourage new customers always to start with a burger, for several reasons. Ground grassfed beef is inexpensive, but carries all the sensational grassfed flavor that distinguishes real beef from factory-farmed meat. Burgers are relatively easy to cook, and since they can be cooked in much the same way as you would handle a conventional burger (with the exception that it is usually safe to let grassfed burgers be a tad more pink in the center), it's the perfect starting place.

---

# ASADO

## (Grilled Short Ribs)

*Asado* has two meanings in Argentina. It is their Spanish word for "grill," but also describes slow-roasted beef short ribs which, according to most Argentineans you speak with, epitomizes the glory of Argentina's ember-roasted offerings. Short ribs are often overlooked here in the United States during grill season. We tend to think of them as "tough cuts," useful only for braises and stews during the winter months. In fact, short ribs had been so rarely purchased by our customers in the past that we'd been known to occasionally use them as dog food...until we traveled down to Argentina and learned just how scrumptious they are. It is true that you might have to chew this meat, and Americans, I've noticed, have a quirky aversion to this notion. But if you roast short ribs on your rotisserie slowly for a minimum of two hours (three is even better if you can monitor the heat and keep it low enough), then season them with *salmeura* and set the table with a good set of steak knives, I *guarantee* you will not be disappointed. If you love grill flavor on your meat, if you like the sweetest perfume of smoke, and relish a deep beefy essence, I think you will join the Argentineans in favoring this cut over any steak or burger. In my estimation, nothing else compares. The consequence, however, is that all the hard-working dogs at Sap Bush Hollow are now rather resentful.

Note: In Argentina a classic *asado* is a long strip of short ribs, cut flanken-style, which can be roasted on a *parilla* (see chapter 6), then cut into individual ribs just before serving. If you have a butcher who will cut them flanken-style, so much the better. However, typically the short ribs in America are cut apart by the butcher. If that's the only way you can buy them, don't worry. Simply spear the meat on your rotisserie as you would kebabs on a skewer, and get grilling. To be faithful to my grilling instructors below the equator, I must admit that we did not use rotisseries to cook *asados* in Argentina, although they are used in neighboring countries. Chapter 6 explains how to cook the ribs using the classic Argentinean style; but when working with American grills, the rotisserie method comes much closer to approximating the grilling conditions of a traditional *parilla*.

*Good for company*
*On a budget*
*Serves 5–6*

**1 batch *salmeura*, see page 50**
**5–6 pounds short ribs, bone-in (allow one pound**
**of ribs per person)**

If using a charcoal grill, light the coals and allow them to burn until they are covered with a layer of gray ash. Pour a line of coals down the left and right side of the grill, and place a drip pan or cast-iron skillet in the center. If cooking with gas, light the front and back burners only. Put your rotisserie attachment in place, spear the meat on the spit (if the ribs are flanken style, thread the spit between every second or third rib, zig-zag). Allow the meat to turn on the spit and slowly roast for 2-3 hours, until the tissue along the exterior of the bones begins to pull away and the meat, when sliced, appears nearly well-done throughout (although there should still be ample juices). As you cook the meat, be sure to leave the lid of the grill open. You want to be sure that the temperature *at the spit*, where the meat is, remains around 300 degrees. To gauge this, you should be able to hold your hand right next to the rotating meat for eight seconds.

Ten minutes before you serve the ribs, splash them liberally with the *salmeura*. Allow them to continue to turn on the rotisserie so that a salty crust forms. When you serve the meat, pass the *salmeura* bottle separately so your guests can add additional sauce as desired.

*If you don't have a rotisserie:* Heat the grill until it is about 300 degrees *at the grate*. This means you should be able to hold your hand just above the metal, almost touching it, for 8 seconds. Set the unseasoned meat bone-side down directly over the flames and allow the meat to roast, uncovered, for about three hours, or until the tissue begins to pull away from the bones and the meat, when sliced, appears nearly well-done throughout. There should still be plenty of juice when you slice it.

During this period, if using charcoal, you will need to pay close attention and add a few coals every few minutes to maintain the grill temperature. Do not flip the short ribs during the initial cooking time. The objective when cooking with this method is to allow the heated *bones*, and not the flames, to gently cook the meat.

Ten minutes before serving, splash the ribs liberally with *salmeura* and allow the meat to continue to cook while the salty crust forms, turning it to be sure the salt solution crusts over all sides. When you serve the meat, pass the *salmeura* separately so your guests can add additional seasoning to taste.

Argentineans often wryly remark, "The rest of the world gets our beef. We get the bones." And it's true. Many of the Argentine cattle ranches are held by the elite class, and much of the beef is exported overseas, where grassfed beef is now claiming a handsome premium. Thus, the highest-quality beef and the most popular cuts, such as the top loin and tenderloin, are very difficult to come by. The top loin cuts that aren't exported, I soon discovered, are of significantly lower quality than the country is capable of producing.

This means that the Argentineans are often left with the most unpopular cuts of beef, most especially the *costillas*, or ribs, which are cross-cut into long ribbons from the front of the chuck. While morsels of *vacio* or *matambre*, flank cuts, grace these South American fires, and thin slices of the round are turned into savory wonders called *milanesas* on the kitchen stove, I believe there is no finer cut of beef turned out of this country than the *costillas*, patiently cooked over the embers in a *parilla*.

I remember the first time our host, Nestor, rode his bicycle to the corner butcher to buy meat for our first asado. Upon return, he proudly presented me with these ribbon-style beef ribs. I smiled politely, my lips pulling tight at the corners of my cheeks as I quietly looked on in horror, wondering how the citizens of this country might enjoy a reputation as aficionados of the flame when they were grilling one of the toughest cuts of meat on the whole beef.

I was in for a surprise. Naturally, after those meats had been grilled for 2–3 hours to medium-well done (one of the few cuts of beef that I advocate grilling until well-done), they did require the use of steak knives, but I've never experienced such genuine, pure, hearty beef flavor. In fact, after years of preferring rib-eyes and top loin steaks, short ribs quickly became my favorite cut of grilled meat.

Despairing, I saw that, in all my years of eating beef, I'd relegated short ribs to heavily seasoned stews and pot roasts (and dog food), never realizing that their true magnificence was to be savored off the fire...so many great grilling opportunities were missed! Even more tragic, consider all the other North Americans who have been deprived of great grill experiences simply because they, too, are conditioned to *eschew the chewy* (that is, all the cuts that are more firmly muscled). When did we learn to expect that we should not have to masticate our food? While the premium cuts of beef such as the tenderloin are prized for their tenderness, they come from parts of the animal that do the least work and, compared to the chewier cuts, have much less beef flavor.

Foreign friends all over the world tell me that they can spot North Americans traveling their city streets by their beautiful, well-cared-for teeth. I suggest that we start using these wondrous devices to enjoy the best meat on the steer. Folks, it's time to start chewing!

# Salmeura

## Argentina (and Brazil's) salt-saturated garlic water

Here you have the single greatest recipe for seasoning grassfed beef. Sure, herby stuff is nice, and spicy stuff is fun. But when you have great flavored beef, this is all you need. This is the one seasoning that should be applied near the end of cooking. Drizzle it over your meat liberally about 10 minutes before it comes off the grill, then flip your cuts around so that the heat will encrust the salt water onto the meat. Once you've tried it on your short ribs, try it on steaks, chicken, pork or lamb.

> 5–6 cloves garlic, finely sliced
> 1 tablespoon black peppercorns, coarsely crushed
> using mortar and pestle
> 1 tablespoon white peppercorns, coarsely crushed
> using mortar and pestle
> 7 tablespoons coarse salt, plus extra
> 1 clean, empty 750 ml wine bottle and cork or
> stopper

Combine the garlic, black and white peppercorns and 2 tablespoons salt in a medium-sized saucepan. Pour in three cups water, then bring the mixture to a rolling boil for 30 seconds. Turn the heat off and allow it to cool for 5 minutes.

Using a funnel, add 3 tablespoons salt to the bottom of the wine bottle. Then pour in the garlic water, including the sliced garlic and ground peppercorns. Cork the bottle. Using your thumb to hold the cork in place, shake vigorously until all the salt is incorporated into the water. Add 2 more tablespoons salt and shake again. If all this salt is absorbed and none has collected on the bottom of the bottle, add additional salt.

In a good salmeura, the water must be *completely* saturated with salt. This means you must continue to add salt and shake until the water will absorb no more and a small pile of salt has gathered on the bottom of the bottle.

Shave off the corner of the cork to allow the mixture to be easily drizzled (we use a pour-spout stopper), then store at room temperature for up to three months, adding more salt, pepper, garlic and hot water to taste to enrich the flavor after each use.

Before applying to the meat, place your bottle of salmeura on the grate of your grill to heat up. For maximum flavor and efficient cooking, always be sure your salmeura is hot before you use it. Once you've splashed it on the meat on your grill, be sure to set the salmeura on the table so that your guests can add more to their meat to taste.

# Short Ribs Marinated
# in Cayenne and Garlic

On rare occasions, for variation, Argentineans will marinate their short ribs before cooking an *asado*. This recipe comes from the Gomez family, who hosted Bob, Saoirse and me during our travels. It is wonderfully fragrant, and not nearly as spicy as you might imagine with all that cayenne pepper!

*Good for company*
*Kid-friendly (surprisingly, this passed the toddler*
    *test!)*
*On a budget*
*Serves 3–5*

4 cloves garlic
1 tablespoon cayenne pepper
1 small onion, peeled and cut in half
1 tablespoon coarse salt
1 tablespoon white peppercorns, coarsely ground
1 tablespoon black peppercorns, coarsely ground
4 tablespoons cognac
4 tablespoons olive oil
4 tablespoons red wine vinegar
4 bay leaves
4 sprigs fresh rosemary
3–5 pounds short ribs

Add the garlic, cayenne, onion, salt, peppercorns, cognac, olive oil and vinegar to the large bowl of a food processor. Purée to make a paste. Rub the paste into the meat, then set the ribs in a plastic bag. Set the bay leaves and rosemary on top, then seal the bag tightly and refrigerate several hours or overnight.

When you are ready to grill, remove the ribs from the bag, but do not blot off the paste. Allow the meat to come to room temperature, then grill as directed in the *asado* recipe above.

### Salsa Criolla and Chimichurri

Often, when Argentina is a chosen subject for foodie magazines, salsa criolla and chimichurri are touted as the quintessential seasonings of the nation, synonymous with the country's famous grassfed beef. However, the more *asadores* and grill fanatics we interviewed, and the deeper we traveled into the country feasting on *asados* in the homes of beef-loving families (rather than in tourist restaurants), the less we saw of these sauces.

While the great *asadores* occasionally serve these sauces for a little variation, when we dined in restaurants, we found that salsa criolla and chimichurri appeared in abundance on the tables where the meat being served was either poorly prepared or slightly rancid. In short, the sauces seemed to be used either to placate tourists or to mask not-so-good beef. Still, they are tasty, and I'd be remiss if after spending so much time in Argentina I failed to give these recipes. These two versions have been handed down for generations in the Gomez family and make splashy accompaniments. If you are working with great beef (which I can only assume you are), consider using these condiments on the meat very lightly—and then having some good tortilla chips on the table to really enjoy their flavor.

# Salsa Criolla

1 red bell pepper, finely diced
1 green bell pepper, finely diced
2 fresh tomatoes, finely diced
1 large onion, finely diced
2 tablespoons red wine vinegar
3 tablespoons olive oil or sunflower oil
1 tablespoon Hungarian paprika
2 cloves garlic, minced
salt and pepper

Combine the bell peppers, tomatoes and onion in a porcelain, stainless steel or other non-reactive bowl. Mix well, then season to taste with salt and pepper. Stir in the vinegar, oil, paprika and garlic. Serve immediately, or refrigerate for an hour while the flavors blend.

# CHIMICHURRI

Occasionally, some folks in Argentina use chimichurri as a marinade for their asados, although this is not a very common practice. Most often it is served on the side as a condiment, to be used very sparingly.

> **1 cup water**
> **1/2 cup red wine vinegar**
> **2 tablespoons fresh oregano, chopped**
> **2 tablespoons fresh parsley, chopped**
> **2 tablespoons fresh thyme, chopped**
> **4 cloves garlic, minced**
> **1/2 teaspoon salt**
> **1/2 teaspoon ground black pepper**
> **1 cup olive oil or sunflower oil**
> **2 bay leaves**

Whisk together the water, vinegar, oregano, parsley, thyme, garlic, salt and pepper. Slowly add the oil, whisking continuously as you pour. Add the bay leaves, stir briefly, then allow the mixture to rest a minimum of 30 minutes before serving, allowing the flavors to incorporate.

# TAMARI-ORANGE WHISKEY KEBABS

When I know we're going to be working late, I like to marinate these kebabs ahead so I can have them ready quickly when we get home. I like to reserve a little extra marinade for brushing on some skewered veggies as an accompaniment.

*Kid-friendly*
*On a budget*
*Serves 6*

1 cup orange juice
3 cloves garlic, minced
1/2 cup bourbon whiskey
1/4 cup olive oil
3 tablespoons Dijon mustard
1/4 cup honey
1/4 cup tamari
1/4 cup cider vinegar
1/2 medium onion, minced
1 tablespoon fresh ginger, minced
2–3 pounds beef kebabs (alternatively, use a
    London broil, sirloin, sirloin tip, top round, or
    eye round, cut into 1 1/2 inch cubes)
metal skewers, or bamboo skewers soaked in
    water for 30 minutes.

Before beginning, take each piece of meat and butterfly it by cutting each cube almost through at the center (this increases the exposure of the meat to the marinade).

In a large stainless-steel, porcelain, glass or other non-reactive bowl, whisk together the orange juice, garlic, whiskey, olive oil, mustard, honey, tamari, vinegar, onion and ginger. Add the cubed meat and mix well to coat. Cover and refrigerate overnight, being sure to stir the kebabs every few hours.

When you are ready to grill, pour off the marinade, blot the meat dry with a paper towel, place it on skewers, and allow the meat to come to room temperature while you prepare the grill.

Heat the grill until the flame is medium-hot. You should be able to hold your hand five inches beyond the flame for no more than 3–5 seconds. Scrape the grate clean with a wire brush, then brush it lightly with oil.

Grill the meat directly over the flame, with the cover in place. Rotate the skewers one-quarter turn every two minutes. After about eight minutes, the meat should be well browned on the outside, but medium-rare in the center. Serve immediately.

---

## A SPECIAL SEASONAL TREAT: GREEN GARLIC

Next to your salt and pepper, garlic has to be the most critical seasoning for the summer grill. Trouble is, garlic isn't in season in most parts of the country until midsummer and fall. Unless you're a wiz at storing your garlic from the prior year's harvest, there's a high likelihood that you'll be confronted with heads of garlic shipped from all over the world. Even our local, organically committed food co-op feels obliged to import garlic from China. While the label on the bulbs touts them as organic, I have a hard time accepting food true to the principles of organic agriculture when it has been shipped across the planet.

The good news is that you don't have to buy it. There is a far more delicious alternative out there. One of the great treats of the late spring and early summer grilling season is green garlic, the early bulbs that are harvested between March and July. These little bulbs with green stalks look something like leeks, but have a lovely mild garlic flavor and a most delightful bright hint of lime. After rinsing the garden grit from these precious wonders, you can use just about the entire plant when cooking. When seasoning meat, you might want to use more than you would if using mature garlic. Green garlic will keep for almost a week when stored in your refrigerator.

---

# BRISKET AND SUDS

Your main job when cooking a brisket is to convert the waxy connective tissue, called collagen, to gelatin, making the meat tender. To accomplish this, it helps to incorporate some moisture into your cooking and to let the internal temperature of the meat slowly rise to over 200 degrees. Cooking a brisket can take hours; if you have a big piece of meat, it can take all day. Of course, such a task offers a prime opportunity to nurse beers (organic, local brews, of course) and avoid chores. However, if you aren't up for a full-day project, then smoke the brisket per the instructions below, but only for two hours. After that, wrap the meat in foil (or set it in an oven-proof casserole with a tight-fitting lid) and roast it in a 300-degree oven until it is fork tender. (This still might take another three hours if you are working with a large piece of brisket.)

*Good for company*
*Kid-friendly*
*On a budget*
*Serves 6-12 (allow 1/2 pound of meat per person)*

1 batch Texas Style Spice Rub, p. 60
1 batch Share-the-Beer Marinade, p. 61
Sweet Tomato Barbecue Sauce, p. 62
1 piece flat-cut brisket, 3–6 lbs (Note: If you wish
    to do an entire brisket, which is considerably
    larger than 3–6 pounds, be sure to double the
    amount of spice rub and marinade you make.)
7 cups mesquite or hickory wood chips or
    chunks, soaked in water. (Note: if you are
    using a gas grill, use only wood chips, not
    chunks. You will only need about 2 cups of
    wood chips in this case.)

The day before you plan to feast, combine the ingredients for the Texas Style Spice Rub and set aside. Whisk together the ingredients for the Share-the-Beer Marinade, reserve one cup, then pour the remainder into a glass, porcelain or stainless-steel bowl. Add the brisket, turn it well to coat, and cover it tightly. Allow the meat to marinate overnight.

On feast day (early in the day), remove the brisket from the marinade and pat it dry. Massage a generous portion of the spice rub into the meat and allow it to come to room temperature. Pour the wood chunks or chips into a bucket of cold water and allow them to soak for a minimum of 30 minutes (ideally longer).

If using charcoal, light your grill, keeping the fire on only one side, and allow it to heat until the cooking chamber is about 200 degrees (a smoking thermometer will be of great help here). Toss a handful of the soaked wood chips or chunks directly on the coals.

If using a gas grill, light the grill, turn all burners to high, then put the soaked wood chips in a foil tray and set it down directly over one burner. Close the lid and pre-heat the cooking chamber (all burners still on high) until smoke billows out. Turn off all but the one burner beneath the wood chips and allow the cooking chamber to come down to 200 degrees (if the chamber won't cool down that low, get it as cool as you can, then plan for a shorter cook time).

Set the brisket in a cast-iron skillet or foil roasting pan and put it on the cool side of the grill. Cover. If using a charcoal grill, open the lid vents and arrange the cover so the vents are directly over the meat—this draws the smoke across the meat.

Barbecue for roughly 1 hour and 10 minutes per pound of meat, basting each hour with the reserved marinade (your cooking time might be less if your gas grill maintains your cooking chamber higher than 200 degrees). On a charcoal grill, the cooking chamber temperature will fluctuate as you burn coals and add more. Be sure never to let the temperature fall below 140 degrees, to safeguard against botulism. Add charcoal as necessary to maintain heat, and wood chips or chunks to maintain smoke. If using a gas grill, be sure you start with ample propane and monitor the gas flow as your thermometer warrants. The meat will be ready when it is fork-tender. Remove it to a platter, carve across the grain and serve with the Sweet Tomato Barbecue Sauce.

# Texas Style Spice Rub

2 tablespoons coarse salt
1 teaspoon ground cumin
3 tablespoons chili powder
2 teaspoons garlic powder
1/4 cup turbinado, sucanat or other unrefined or
    partially refined sugar
1/2 teaspoon cayenne pepper (optional)
1 tablespoon ground black pepper

Add all the above ingredients to a small bowl and mix well.

# SHARE-THE-BEER MARINADE

It never hurts to appease the Gods of Barbecue by offering a little beer to the brisket. Leave out the Tabasco if you don't like spicy food.

> 24 ounces beer
> 1/2 cup molasses
> 1-2 teaspoons Tabasco sauce
> 3 tablespoons Texas-Style Spice Rub, above
> 1/2 cup cider vinegar

Add all the above ingredients to a stainless steel or other non-reactive bowl. Whisk well.

# Sweet Tomato Barbecue Sauce

1 tablespoon butter
1 medium onion, finely chopped
1 cup strong black coffee
3 cloves garlic, minced
1/2 cup honey
1/2 cup cider vinegar
4 tablespoons tomato paste
2 tablespoons honey mustard
1 teaspoon salt
1 teaspoon freshly ground black pepper

Melt the butter in a saucepan over a medium flame. Add the onions and sauté until translucent. Stir in the remaining ingredients and allow the sauce to simmer, uncovered, until lightly thickened, about 20 minutes. If desired, season to taste with additional honey, vinegar, salt and pepper. Serve warm. If refrigerated in an airtight container, the sauce will keep several weeks.

# JAVA-CINNAMON SMOKED CHUCK ROAST

If you like to linger around your barbecue even as the days grow short, here's one last thrill for the grill that tastes great as summer wanes and the flavors of fall start to tempt your palate.

*Good for company*
*Kid-friendly*
*On a budget*
*Serves 6–8*

1 batch Java-Cinnamon Spice Rub (page 65)
1 batch Coffee Molasses Mop (page 65)
1 boneless chuck eye roast (or other boneless
    chuck roast), 3–4 pounds
7 cups maple or hickory wood chips or chunks,
    soaked in water. (Note: If you are using a gas
    grill, use only wood chips, not chunks. You
    will only need about 2 cups of wood chips in
    this case.)

The day before you plan to cook your roast, massage all but 1/4 cup of the Java-Cinnamon Spice Rub into the meat. Wrap it in plastic and refrigerate overnight. About 8 or 9 hours before you are ready to eat, remove the meat and allow it to come to room temperature. Meanwhile, prepare the Coffee Molasses Mop per the directions below, then prepare your grill.

If using charcoal, light your grill, keeping the fire on only one side, and allow it to heat until the cooking chamber is about 200 degrees (a smoking thermometer will be of great help here). Toss a handful of the soaked wood chips or chunks directly on the coals.

If using a gas grill, light the grill, turn all burners to high, then put all the soaked wood chips in a foil tray and set it down directly over one burner. Close the lid and preheat the cooking chamber (all burners still on high) until smoke billows out. Turn off all but the one burner beneath the wood chips and allow the cooking chamber to come down to 200 degrees (if the chamber won't cool that low, get it as cool as you can and plan for a shorter cook time).

Place the chuck roast in a large cast-iron skillet (or disposable roasting pan) on the side opposite the fire. Close the grill lid. If you are using a charcoal grill, arrange the lid so that the vents are partially open and on the same side as the meat in order to draw the smoke through. Monitor the temperature of the smoking chamber throughout the day, making sure it stays around 200 degrees. (If you are using a charcoal barbecue, you will occasionally have to add more coals to maintain the fire, and wood chips or chunks to maintain the smoke. For safety, be sure the cooking chamber never falls below 140 degrees.)

Allow the roast to smoke for about four hours, being sure to baste it with the Coffee Molasses Mop every time you lift the grill lid. Then, make the fire hotter, allowing the cooking chamber to come up to 400 degrees. Pour any remaining mop into the bottom of the pan, cover it with aluminum foil, put the grill lid back down, and allow the meat to cook an additional 3 hours, or until it is fork-tender (this finishing can also take place in the oven, if you'd rather, using a covered dish). Remove the roast from the heat and allow it to rest about 10 minutes, loosely tented with the foil.

Carve the meat and arrange it on a platter, and serve the pan juices on the side.

# Java-Cinnamon Spice Rub

2 tablespoons ground coffee
2 tablespoons chili powder
2 teaspoons ground black pepper
2 tablespoons coarse sea salt
2 tablespoons ground cinnamon
2 tablespoons granulated maple sugar (or sucanat,
    turbinado or other unrefined or partially
    refined sugar)

Add all the above ingredients to a small bowl and blend well.

# Coffee Molasses Mop

2 cups strong black coffee
1/4 cup Java-Cinnamon Spice Rub (above)
1/2 cup molasses
1 cinnamon stick

Whisk together the coffee, spice rub and molasses in a medium saucepan on your stovetop. Add the cinnamon stick, turn the heat on to medium, and allow the mixture to come to a boil, stirring often. Reduce the heat to low and allow the mop to simmer for about 20 minutes.

## LITTLE-KNOWN AND LUSCIOUS: THE CHUCK EYE

How very sad that the noble chuck, the most flavorful primal of a beef, is often regarded as the "junk meat," the source of "hamburger grinds!" While I could easily write an entire volume devoted to this prince of the primals (Prince Chuck?), I want to call your attention to one particularly spectacular cut.

The chuck eye, also referred to as the boneless chuck filet, boneless chuck roll, chuck tender or Scotch tender, is a continuation of the rib-eye meat that extends to the front part of a beef. It is not quite as tender as the rib-eye or prime rib, but it is *darn* close. In fact, a slow-roasted boneless chuck eye roast that doesn't exceed medium-rare has been passed off as prime rib in more than a few restaurants that won't swing the price for the real thing.

The beauty of the chuck eye is that, in addition to having all the fantastic flavor that comes from the stronger muscles of the animal, it is also extremely versatile. With indoor cooking, it is the most tender of pot roasts, *and* it can be slowly oven-roasted. On the grill, this beautifully marbled, juicy hunk of meat is luscious off the spit and equally delicious after a long, slow smoke. And the best part? The price! Prime-rib quality at a chuck price is hard to beat.

# ROSEMARY STUDDED
# SPIT-ROASTED BEEF

Don't pass over those beautiful beef roasts on display at your farmers' market just because it's summer. If you're looking to create a great grilled-beef experience for a crowd, without a lot of expense, this makes a lovely, elegant feast, especially if you serve it with a horseradish cream sauce. I like this roast best off the rotisserie, but you can also prepare it using the indirect cooking method.

*Elegant*
*Good for company*
*On a budget*
*Serves 6–8*

**1/4 cup fresh rosemary leaves**
**3 cloves garlic, slivered**
**2 tablespoons coarse salt**
**1 tablespoon ground black pepper**
**1 round roast (top, bottom or eye round), or**
    **sirloin roast, approximately 3-4 pounds**

Cut a series of 1/2-inch-deep holes all over the surface of the meat, each about 2 inches apart. If there is a layer of fat, be sure the cut is deep enough to reach the muscle tissue beneath it. Insert the fresh rosemary leaves and a sliver of garlic in each hole, then rub the salt and pepper all over the roast.

If using the indirect cooking method, heat one side of the grill with the lid down until the chamber is about 200 degrees. If using a rotisserie on a gas grill, preheat the grill by using the front and rear burners. If using a rotisserie on a charcoal grill, light the coals and then rake them into two rows, leaving a gap down the center. Be sure to place a drip pan under the meat if using a rotisserie. Regardless of your method, cook the meat with the grill lid down.

Monitor the temperature of the cooking chamber, being sure to add more coals or adjust the flame to keep the temperature between 200 and 250 degrees. The internal temperature of the finished meat should be 125 degrees for medium-rare. Estimated cooking time will be approximately 40 minutes per pound. To serve, carve the meat very thinly and, if you like, offer horseradish cream sauce.

Note: Sometimes grills and circumstances are uncooperative in allowing you to keep the temperature of the cooking chamber cool enough, particularly with the lid down. Since you are not trying to smoke the meat, in this instance, it is fine to remove the lid if you are using a rotisserie. If you are using the indirect method, get the chamber as cool as you can, then carefully monitor the internal temperature of the meat and the chamber. If necessary, you can periodically remove the grill lid for a few moments if there is too much heat buildup.

*To make your own horseradish cream sauce:* Horseradish sauce is one of the easiest condiments in the world to prepare. Simply add 1 cup of sour cream to a bowl, then stir in prepared horseradish to taste. I usually use about 3-4 tablespoonfuls if the jar is newly opened (when the horseradish will be most piquant), but I add much more if I have been storing it in my fridge for a while. To find the right heat for you, taste frequently as you add the horseradish. If you don't have sour cream, you can also whip 8 ounces of unseasoned heavy cream until stiff peaks form, then fold in the horseradish.

## HOW DO FARMERS TAKE CARE OF
## GRASSFED ANIMALS IN WINTER?

Anyone with even the slightest mind for math and weather patterns can see this conundrum: A farmer sells grassfed beef. The animals are processed at an age between 18-29 months. Nowhere in the U.S.A. does the grass grow productively year-round. In the height of summer, the grasses die off down south. In the depths of winter, deep snows and cold temperatures cause grass in the north to go dormant. So how do we do it?

There are a few options. Some farmers winter-feed their cattle something called *haylage*, grass silage stored in an upright silo or bunker silo, or *bailage*, forage (grass) that is baled at a higher moisture content than dry hay, then wrapped in plastic for storage. The grasses stored in these ways ferment and produce an acid that preserves them. The result is a highly digestible, nutritious dinner. Some farmers, interested in keeping their livestock on fresh green grass year-round, ship their cattle around the country, sending them to grazing camps during different seasons, to ensure continuous access to pasture that is in a state of optimal growth and nutrition. Both of these techniques result in beef that fatten, or "finish," relatively quickly, although at considerable expense. Since these methods also require more intensive use of fossil fuels—through harvesting and plastic wrapping bailage, or in the transport of cattle, many farmers simply "carry over" their cattle on traditional hay, then finish them on grass once the fields turn lush and green again. This third method takes the longest time, but it has the least overall environmental impact and, though the cattle are usually a bit older, the meat is every bit as delicious.

# BURGUNDY CHUCK ROAST

Marinades are wonderful for what might otherwise be called "the tougher" cuts of meat, like chucks and rounds. Many people think this is because marinades tenderize the meat, but they don't. In fact, if left in a marinade for too long, the meat turns gray and mushy. The real reasons "the tougher cuts" fare so well with marinating is because they are less inclined to turn mushy and they have more robust flavor, which means the great beefy taste will shine through even if your marinade seasonings penetrate deeply through the meat. Like the Rosemary-Studded Beef, this dish also pairs well with horseradish cream sauce. See p. 68 for instructions on how to prepare it.

*Good for company*
*On a budget*
*Serves 4-10*

2 tablespoons coarse salt
2 teaspoons ground black pepper
4 cups burgundy or other dry red wine
1 onion, minced
2 cloves garlic, minced
1/4 cup fresh parsley, coarsely chopped
1 tablespoon fresh thyme leaves
1 (2–5 pound) chuck eye roast, top round, bottom
     round or eye round.

Press the salt and pepper into the surface of the beef. Set aside. Combine the wine, onion, garlic, parsley and thyme in a glass, porcelain or stainless-steel bowl. Mix well. Add the beef and turn it until it is well moistened. Allow the meat to bathe in the marinade for 6 hours at room temperature, or overnight in the refrigerator, being sure to turn it occasionally.

Start a medium-sized fire in your grill. If using a rotisserie, rake the coals (or light the gas burners) on either side of where the spit will turn. If using the indirect method, light only one side of the grill. Cover the grill and allow the cooking chamber to come up to about 250 degrees.

Remove the roast from the marinade and pat it dry. If using a rotisserie, slide the meat onto the spit and put it in place over the grate. If using the indirect method, set the meat on the side of the grill that is not lit. Keep the cooking chamber between 225 and 275 degrees, cooking about 1 hour per pound of meat, removing the meat when the internal temperature is between 125 and 140 degrees.

Note: Sometimes grills and circumstances are uncooperative in allowing you to keep the temperature of the cooking chamber cool enough, particularly with the lid down. Since you are not trying to smoke the meat, in this instance, it is fine to remove the lid if you are using a rotisserie. If you are using the indirect method, get the chamber as cool as you can, then carefully monitor the internal temperature of the meat and the chamber. If necessary, you can periodically remove the grill lid for a few moments if there is too much heat buildup.

# BEEF VINDALOO

We have a tendency to disregard braising dishes during the summer, assuming that they are typical "winter fare." Tsk-tsk. This is a culinary waste, because meats braised over a fire are enhanced by the smoke. They will result in exotic dishes that could never be duplicated on a kitchen stove. Plus, you get to keep the heat out of the house! Beef Vindaloo (or *bife vindalho*) is a common dish from India that goes well with rice and all those fresh garden vegetables, stir-fried and tossed lightly with yogurt and seasoned with a touch of coriander, cumin, salt, pepper and curry powder.

*Elegant*
*Good for company*
*Kid-friendly*
*On a budget*
*Serves 4*

1 teaspoon mustard seeds
3–6 dried red chili peppers, crumbled
1 tablespoon whole cumin seeds
1 tablespoon black peppercorns
2 tablespoons fresh ginger, grated
3 cloves garlic, crushed
1 teaspoon turmeric
3 teaspoons fine sea salt
1/2 cup cider vinegar
4 tablespoons butter
6 onions, finely sliced
1 quart chicken broth
1–2 teaspoons tamarind paste
1–3 teaspoons honey
2 pounds stew beef
steamed rice
2 cups maple, apple or hickory wood chips or
    chunks, soaked in water (if using a gas grill,
    use only the chips)

Combine the mustard seeds, crumbled chili peppers, cumin and peppercorns in a spice grinder and grind to make a fine powder. Pour the powder into a stainless-steel or porcelain bowl, then whisk in the ginger, garlic, turmeric, 2 teaspoons salt and vinegar. Add the stew beef and mix thoroughly to be sure it is well coated.

If cooking with charcoal, light a large hot fire on one side of your grill, then toss a handful of wood chips or chunks over the coals and set the grate in place.

If using a gas grill, light the grill, turn all burners to high, then put all the soaked wood chips in a foil tray and set it down directly over one burner. Close the lid and preheat the cooking chamber (all burners still on high) until smoke billows out.

Set a Dutch oven (heavy cast-iron casserole dish) directly over the hottest part of the grill. Allow it to heat up, then add the butter. Once the butter bubbles down, add the onions and the remaining teaspoon of salt. Cook, stirring often, until the onions have melted down and caramelized, about 25–30 minutes (try to keep the grill covered between stirs to preserve the smoke).

Drain any excess liquid off the beef, then add it to the Dutch oven and stir well. Pour in the chicken broth. Stir again, then put the grill lid in place. If you are working with a gas grill and the smoke has petered out, you might need to remove the Dutch oven temporarily and repeat the instructions above, to build up more smoke before you resume cooking the meat. If you are working with charcoal, simply add more wet wood chips or chunks to the embers.

Allow the mixture to simmer 45 minutes to one hour, until the meat is tender, occasionally adding coals and wood chips or chunks as necessary to maintain adequate heat and smoke. When the meat is tender, promptly remove it from the grill, stir in the tamarind paste and honey to taste, and serve with the steamed rice.

# WHY IS GRASSFED MEAT SO EXPENSIVE?

It's not. At least, I don't think so. To say something is expensive is a purely subjective matter. Recently, my husband, who grew up in a sailing family, found an advertisement for a used sailboat. "That's really a great buy," he exclaimed, briefly forgetting our agrarian income. A land-loving girl who regards boating as an exercise in water survival and marital tolerance, I looked at the ad and scoffed, "That's outrageously expensive!"

The same subjectivity applies to food. A recent research trip to our local grocery store revealed that a box of Berry Burst Cheerios was double the price of a dozen Sap Bush Hollow Farm pastured eggs. No name, factory-farmed, slimy boneless chicken breasts cost more per pound than a whole fresh chicken from our farm, and a bag of potato chips costs, per pound, almost as much as a pound of grassfed ground beef. An examination of our local Burger King menu indicated that four "value meals" (two of them child portions) would cost about $24; but an organic, local dinner for four from our farmers' market including chicken, baked potatoes and fresh broccoli would only cost $20—and it would yield leftovers for salads or casseroles, a carcass for chicken soup stock, and scraps for the dog! From this perspective, Berry Burst Cheerios, factory-farmed chicken breasts, potato chips and Burger King are all expensive. Furthermore, in addition to the prices we pay at the grocery store or restaurant, we've already paid for these foods (even if we don't buy them!) with our tax dollars through farm subsidies—agricultural programs that don't apply to pasture-based producers. What's more, the use of antibiotics and hormone implants in factory meats leads to many health costs that go unaccounted for.

It should not be the job of pasture-based farmers to find ways to make their prices lower to compete with factory-farmed meats. Most of the prices I've seen farmers charging show honest pricing that reflects the real costs of their products with a fair margin for a very modest living. And, frankly, I can't help but bristle when a well-heeled professional looks at my display at a farmers' market and, with an accusatory tone, opines that our meats are "too expensive." It suggests that my family doesn't deserve a fair return for the labor, careful attention and genuine devotion we put into our work.

While locally raised grassfed meats *seem* to be pricier than factory-farmed meat produced by large multinational food corporations, I learned through our meat adventures in Europe and South America that most pastured meat prices in this country are actually close to the normal cost of meats in other countries. It is ironic that our country, with one of the highest standards of living in the world, places such a high priority on keeping food cheap. Put another way, we seem to put a very low value on our food. We'll balk at paying $15 for a chicken, but think nothing of paying $60 for a month of cable television; $80 for mobile telecommunications, *and* $100 for a few meals at chain restaurants.

Rather than making food affordable by making it "cheap," perhaps we should address the greater problem of securing living wages for working people, enabling them to afford *good* food, a pot to cook in and time to cook, and shifting priorities so people decide to pay the real cost of their food. My bet is that most of us would find our bank accounts would look healthier with a locally based clean-food diet. After all, with clean, healthy food, we're bound to spend less money on the medical system!

## CHAPTER THREE

# *Lamb*

Long before there were beef roaming the hills of Sap Bush Hollow, before the broilers and pigs and guard dogs and geese and guinea hens filled the fields and valleys with their calls...there were the sheep. My dad grew up on a farm in New Jersey, where his folks raised beef. As a toddler the big animals scared him, and he pestered his parents for sheep, "because they were my size," he adds. And so, on his third birthday, his dad led him out to the barn and presented him with three lambs.

My dad was never again without a flock. Nor was my grandfather, for that matter. At eighty-eight years old, Grandpa Hayes still goes out to tend several hundred ewes every morning, all descended from those first three lambs. Despite all the other livestock, the sheep remain the center of every Hayes farmer's heart. Maybe this is still owing to our size—the tallest Hayes is only five foot nine, and most of us fall well below that mark. We move about our sheep with comfort and confidence, yet approach our steers with much more caution. Every successful farm is a marriage between the unique attributes of the land, the farmers, and the crops or livestock they choose to work with. Our steep hillsides at Sap Bush Hollow are perilous for crop production, but paradise for grazing sheep; and our stocky bodies seem to match the landscape, enabling us to scramble up the steep pastures with ease, move the fences, and tend to the newborns. We have learned to tend chickens, to work with beef, to negotiate with pigs. But at the end of the day, we will always be sheep people.

Especially at the dinner table. We take our lamb very seriously. Whole lambs are cooked on a spit for graduation parties, crown roasts adorn the table for Christmas dinner, succulent legs are presented at Easter and birthdays, and slow-smoked riblets glazed with maple syrup and mustard are a favorite midday feast. Our customers are equally enamored with these tender morsels of meat. And that's good news for them. Like beef, lamb is rich in easily digestible macro and trace minerals, fat soluble vitamins, B12, and carnitine, a vitamin-like substance critical to healthy heart function (1). We have only one real problem producing this meat: nearly always, after processing lamb, our stocks are depleted within a day or two. If there is one meat that we can never keep in adequate supply, it is our lamb.

Thus, quite surprising to my family, the American Sheep Industry Association reports that lamb consumption in the United States is extremely low, around 1.1 pounds per person annually. An article posted on Meatnews.com talks about product development efforts aimed at increasing lamb marketability in the United States and Canada. Some of the new items appearing in grocery stores include pre-seasoned frozen mini-skewers, pre-seasoned and frozen lamb burgers, and fully cooked lamb sold in microwavable trays (2). I don't know any grassfed lamb producers who feel it necessary to pre-season their lamb and sell it already affixed to skewers. Nor do we farmers need to market it precooked or packaged as a ready-to-eat meal. When lamb is raised in an authentic environment by people who love sheep, it sells itself.

1. S. Fallon, M. Enig, *Nourishing Traditions*, New Trends Publishing, 1999.
2. "Global Team Works to Increase Lamb Consumption," Meatnews.com, May 2006.

# Classic Lamb Chops

Some grilling books advocate searing lamb chops over high heat before moving them to a cooler flame, but grassfed lamb tends to be less fatty, causing fewer flare-ups. This means that your chops can be grilled directly over the fire. If you are cooking loin or rib chops, allow 2 chops per person. If you are preparing shoulder chops, usually one chop per person is ample. There are loads of fun seasonings for lamb chops, but I find the delicate flavors are best served by a little garlic, salt, pepper and olive oil.

*Elegant*
*Minimal preparation*
*Kid-friendly (particularly rib chops, which are not*
*only sized nicely for little fingers, but which*
*offer a tasty bone that is fun to chew on)*
*Serves 4*

**2 cloves garlic, slivered**
**2-3 tablespoons olive oil**
**coarse salt, to taste**
**fresh ground pepper, to taste**
**8 loin or rib chops, 1 1/4-inch thick; or 4 shoulder**
**chops, 1 1/4-inch thick**

With a sharp knife, slice a series of tiny slits into both sides of each chop. Slip a sliver of garlic into each slit. Brush each chop lightly with olive oil, then sprinkle with salt and pepper. Allow the meat to come to room temperature while you light the grill.

Once your flame is medium-hot and you can hold your hand 5 inches above the grate for about 4 seconds, brush the grate clean, then grill the chops, covered, 4-6 minutes per side until they achieve the desired doneness, between 120 and 145 degrees.

## CHOOSING YOUR CHOPS

There are primarily three different types of lamb chops, all suitable for grilling. The **loin chops** are the most lean and contain a piece of the tenderloin, making them the lamb equivalent of a beef T-bone or porterhouse steak. The smaller portion of meat on one side will be fine-grained and tender, while the larger side will be slightly more lean and chewy.

If you like your lamb crusted with a delicate layer of crispy fat, then opt for the **rib chops.** Because they are slightly fattier, they are often juicier and more flavorful than the loin cuts. If price and flavor are your main concerns, choose the **shoulder chops**. Higher in collagen, these are slightly chewier than ribs or loins, but also have much more flavor and wonderful marbling. They cost less, too. Shoulders are great cuts for braising, but grassfed lamb is typically harvested young before the "tough cuts" (like shoulder pieces) actually get tough, so these chops are actually quite tender.

# Sesame Grilled Lamb Chops

If you're looking for a new twist for your lamb chops, try this gentle marinade for fun flavor that won't overpower the meat. I like to serve these with Tamari Ginger Buckwheat Noodles, so I've included the recipe on page 82.

*Elegant*
*Kid-friendly*
*Serves 2*

1 large clove garlic, minced
1/2 cup orange juice
1 teaspoon ground ginger
1/8 teaspoon cayenne pepper
2 tablespoons tamari
1/4 cup fresh chives, diced
4 tablespoons toasted sesame oil
4 loin or rib chops, 1 1/4-inch thick; or 2 shoulder
    chops, 1 1/4-inch thick

Whisk together the garlic, orange juice, ginger, cayenne, tamari, chives and 2 tablespoons of the sesame oil. Pour into a shallow bowl or large zip-lock bag. Add the chops and turn to coat. Allow the meat to marinate, turning once, for 1–2 hours.

Light the grill and allow it to heat up for about 5 minutes with the cover in place. Once the flames are medium-hot and you can hold your hand 5 inches above the grate for no more than 4 seconds, scrape the grate clean.

Remove the chops from the marinade and blot dry. Brush them with the remaining sesame oil, then grill directly over the fire with the grill cover on, 4–6 minutes per side until they achieve the desired doneness (120–145 degrees). If desired, serve on a bed of Tamari Ginger Buckwheat Noodles.

## IS YOUR LAMB TOO CHEWY?

Lamb is one of the few meats that many Americans are willing to eat blood-rare. However, if you are cooking your chops until they are just rare, and occasionally find they are a little tough, don't be afraid to toss them back on the grill for a few more moments. Unlike traditional rare-cooked beef steaks, which get tougher as they're cooked further, very rare lamb becomes *more* tender if carefully brought to medium-rare.

# TAMARI GINGER BUCKWHEAT NOODLES

Ok, ok, it's not a lamb recipe…but it goes so well with the Sesame Grilled Lamb Chops!!

*Elegant*
*Kid-friendly*
*On a budget*
*Serves 4*

**1/4 cup tamari**
**2 tablespoons Mirin or sherry**
**2 tablespoons honey**
**8 ounces dried buckwheat soba noodles**
**4 green onions, finely sliced**
**2 tablespoons grated ginger root**
**1 tablespoon sesame oil**

Fill a 2-quart saucepan halfway with water and bring to a boil. Add the soba. When the water returns to a boil, add 1 cup cold water. Once it returns to a boil again, add an additional 1 cup cold water. Bring the water to a boil once more, then test for doneness. Noodles should be *al dente*. If necessary boil 1–2 minutes longer.

Drain the noodles, then rinse them in cold water. Pour them into a medium-sized bowl and toss with the sesame oil. Whisk together the tamari, Mirin, honey, and ginger, then add the mixture to the noodles. Toss well to coat. Garnish with the green onions. Serve cold or at room temperature.

# RACK OF LAMB WITH A SPICED FIG CRUST

This was a fun recipe to make, and it earned a resounding "Good recipe, Mommy!" from the two-year-old of the house.

*Elegant*
*Kid-friendly*
*Serves 4*

1/4 cup dried figs, finely chopped (any variety
    will work)
1/4 cup brandy
1/4 cup water
1 teaspoon ground cumin
1 tablespoon ground coriander
1 tablespoon coarse salt
2 teaspoons ground cinnamon
1/4 – 1/2 teaspoon cayenne pepper
1/4 teaspoon ground cloves
2 cloves garlic
2 tablespoons olive oil
2 racks of lamb (2–4 pounds total)

Simmer the figs in the brandy and water until all the liquid has been absorbed by the fruit. Add the mixture, along with the spices, salt, garlic and olive oil, to a food processor and purée to make a paste. Rub the paste into the meat. If the backbone has been pre-cut, work the paste between the ribs as much as possible. Cover with plastic and allow the meat to marinate 2 hours or overnight before preparing the grill.

Light one side of the grill and allow it to warm up until it is medium-hot (you should be able to hold your hand 5 inches above the grate for no more than 4 seconds). Scrape the grate clean with a wire brush, then lay the meat bone-side up directly over the heat. Grill until nicely browned, about 5–7 minutes. Using tongs, turn the racks so that each side (including the ends) has an opportunity to brown over the flames. Once the meat is nicely browned, insert an internal meat thermometer into the center, then lay the racks, bone-side down, on the cool side of the grill. Set the cover in place and grill 10–15 minutes longer, until the internal temperature is 120–145 degrees.

Transfer the racks to a cutting board and allow them to rest before carving.

## HOW TO CARVE A RACK OF LAMB

Ideally, before you purchase a rack of lamb, your farm's butcher has removed or sliced through the chine bone, making it easier to cut through the individual chops with a heavy carving knife. However, this isn't always the case. If you find that you cannot easily cut through the chops, do not reach for your ax or chainsaw—it would disrupt the harmony of your dinner.

Instead, take a deep breath, then after allowing guests to admire your lovely roast, surreptitiously slip back into the kitchen and set the meat, fat-side-up, on a cutting board. Starting at the thin end, use a sharp, narrow knife and gently slice the entire piece off the length of the rib rack, keeping the knife blade just above the bone. Continue to trace along the bottom of the roast, removing the meat as one solid piece. Set the bones aside, then carve the meat cross-wise into thin slices.

Once your guests are nearing the end of dinner, you can slip back into the kitchen under the auspices of preparing dessert and coffee, seize the skeletal remains, yank the bones apart and gnaw off all the sweet meat that was left behind, being sure to swab the telltale grease from your cheeks before returning with the coffee cups.

# MINT SPICED LAMB BURGERS

Tired of ordinary burgers? These lamb burgers have a bright, memorable flavor. Instead of smothering them in a bun, consider serving them in a lightly toasted pita bread with a yogurt mint sauce (p. 87).

Seasoning note: Garam Masala lends a lovely hint of the exotic Far East to this recipe. However, if you can't find it or don't feel like making it (a recipe for the famous spice blend follows), don't let the lack of this ingredient dissuade you from the recipe. The burgers will be just as lovely without it; the flavor will simply be more herby.

*Minimal preparation*
*Kid-friendly*
*On a budget*
*Serves 4-5*

1/2 onion, finely minced
1 teaspoon salt
4 ounces *chevre* (soft goats' milk cheese)
1 cup fresh mint, finely chopped
1/2 cup fresh cilantro, finely chopped
1 small chili pepper, diced (seeds and white
     membrane removed)
2 cloves garlic, crushed
2 tablespoons Garam Masala (p. 87)
1 1/2 pounds ground lamb

Add all the above ingredients to a large bowl and mix well. You may need to use your hands to be sure the ingredients are sufficiently blended.

Loosely shape the meat into 4 or 5 meatballs, then flatten each ball until it is just shy of one-inch thick. With your fingertips, make a small well in the top of each patty to prevent the meat from getting puffy over the flames. Set the patties aside while you light the grill and brush off the cooking grate.

When the grill is medium-hot and you can hold your hand 5 inches above it for no more than 4 seconds, brush the grill down lightly with vegetable oil, then set the patties directly over the flame with the well facing up. Grill, covered, about 4–5 minutes per side for medium burgers.

# Garam Masala

Garam Masala is a wonderful seasoning for lamb, beef, pork or poultry. It is available pre-packaged at Indian stores and often in well-stocked grocery stores. It is also available through mail order over the Internet. If you prefer to make your own, here is a simple recipe.

**1 (5-inch) cinnamon stick, broken into pieces**
**6 black cardamom pods**
**8 green cardamom pods**
**1 teaspoon whole cloves**
**2 teaspoons whole cumin seeds**
**3 teaspoons whole black peppercorns**
**2 teaspoons whole fennel seeds**
**4 bay leaves, torn into pieces**

Heat a skillet over a medium flame, then add all the ingredients. Dry roast the spices, stirring often, until they are fragrant and lightly browned. Store in an airtight jar and grind just prior to using. (I keep a spare coffee grinder on hand just for this purpose.)

# Yogurt Mint Sauce

**1/2 cup fresh mint**
**1 1/2 teaspoons fresh ginger, grated**
**1/2 cup plain, whole milk yogurt**
**salt to taste**

Place the mint and ginger in a food processor and chop until a dry paste forms. Whisk the mixture into the yogurt, then add salt to taste. Serve immediately, or refrigerate in an airtight container.

## SO WHAT IS "SPRING LAMB" ANYWAY?

In France, *agneau de lait*, suckling lamb, is what *some* Americans have been known to call *spring lamb*. This is lamb that was harvested before it was weaned, and it is usually cooked whole on the spit. *Agneau*, also called *spring lamb*, is young, weaned lamb, ranging in weight anywhere from 20–50 pounds, depending on which authorities you consult. Hothouse lamb is raise indoors, usually weighs 15–20 pounds live, and is used to accommodate the various Easter-season holidays from different religious traditions.

However, when lambs are born and raised on grass, in certain parts of the country the "spring" lamb won't be available until summer or fall.

Confused yet?

Here's a way to make it simple:

Spring lamb: Any lamb that is younger than eight months old.

Lamb: Lamb that is between eight and thirteen months old.

Yearling lamb: Lamb that is between thirteen and twenty months old.

Mutton: Sheep that is two years old or more.

Ram: Big, randy boy sheep.

Ewe: Big mommy sheep.

Eew: What most Americans say when served mutton or ram.

While various epicureans might have their own ideas and definitions about just how "spring" a spring lamb should be, for those of us who enjoy great food more than specific terminology, the most important distinction is that of flavor. Grassfed lamb has a natural sweetness and a more delicate, less "gamey" flavor than grain-fed lamb. However, flavor intensity will vary with breed and age. As a rule: the younger the lamb, the more mild the flavor; the older the lamb, the more assertive the taste. My personal preference is for yearling lamb, where the distinctive characteristics of the meat are pronounced but not overpowering. At Sap Bush Hollow Farm, where lambing occurs in pastures around May, that means that my favorite one-year-old lamb is available in...are you ready for this? *The Spring*.

When you visit your farmer, remember that they are unlikely to make these various distinctions in their lamb products. Rather, what will be available is the lamb that was ready for harvest at that time of year—be it spring lamb, lamb, or yearling lamb. Mutton, however, is usually labeled separately and is definitely worth sampling.

# ASADO-STYLE LAMB RIBS

The ribs, a.k.a. riblets, breast of lamb, or spare ribs, are my favorite part of the lamb—rich in flavor, with the perfect balance of fat and lean meat. These are the cheapest cuts of lamb you can buy, but beyond a doubt, one of the finest. I learned this simple method for preparing them while studying with Nestor Gomez in Argentina.

*Kid-friendly*
*On a budget*
*Serves 4*

**Salmeura, p. 50**
**2 slabs lamb riblets (also called breast of lamb),**
    **1 1/2–2 pounds each**

Light a hot fire in your gas or charcoal grill, but leave the lid off, allowing the heat to quickly dissipate. You should be able to hold your hand over the grate, at the height of the meat, for eight seconds. If you have a grill thermometer, the grilling temperature at the grate should be 300 degrees.

Lay the meat directly over the flame, bone-side down. The intent here is to let the fire heat the bones, and then to allow the bones to cook the meat.

Grill the ribs a minimum of 2 hours, maintaining the temperature at the grate around 300 degrees. When the meat is ready to eat, it will pull away from the bone and, when sliced, it should be tender. Lamb riblets, cooked properly, will be well-done to guarantee tenderness.

Ten minutes before removing them from the grill, splash the meat liberally with the salmeura. Flip ribs briefly so that the fire will help the salt solution to crust over the meat. Cut the ribs apart and pass them with the bottle of salmeura so your guests may add more seasoning to taste.

# Maple Mustard Smoked Lamb Riblets

Many people enjoy rare lamb, but when working with riblets, the meat should be well-done, as it will be more tender and less chewy. Thus, a long slow cook in the smoker has magnificent results.

*Good for company*
*Kid-friendly*
*On a budget*
*Serves 4*

**1/2 cup maple syrup**
**1/4 cup Dijon mustard**
**salt and pepper to taste**
**2 slabs lamb riblets (breast of lamb), 1 1/2–2**
    **pounds each**
**Several handfuls of hickory or maple woodchips**
    **or chunks, soaked in water for at least 30 min-**
    **utes. (If you are cooking with gas, use only**
    **chips.)**

Whisk together the maple syrup and the mustard. Liberally brush the mixture on both sides of the ribs, reserving a small amount for glazing the meat later. Sprinkle the slabs generously with salt and pepper on both sides. Allow the meat to come to room temperature while you prepare the grill.

If using charcoal, light your grill, keeping the fire on only one side, and allow it to heat until the cooking chamber is about 225–250 degrees (a smoking thermometer will be of great help here). Toss a handful of the soaked wood chips or chunks directly on the coals.

If using a gas grill, light the grill, turn all burners to high, then put all the soaked wood chips in a foil tray and set it down directly over one burner. Close the lid and preheat the cooking chamber (all burners still on high) until smoke billows out. Turn off all but the one burner beneath the wood chips and allow the cooking chamber to come down to 225–250 degrees. If the chamber won't cool down that low, get it as low as you can, then plan for a shorter cook time.

Lay the riblets, bone-side down, on the cool side of the grill. Cover. If using a charcoal grill, open the lid vents and arrange the cover so that the vents are directly over the meat, drawing the smoke through the chamber.

Smoke the meat about 4 hours, maintaining the temperature of the cooking chamber between 225 and 300 degrees, averaging around 250 degrees. When the riblets are ready, the meat will be pulling away from the bone and, when sliced, the meat will be tender. Quickly brush the slabs with one last layer of the maple mustard glaze, and allow them to smoke ten minutes longer before serving.

# ROTISSERIED LEG OF LAMB STUFFED WITH APRICOTS AND CHERRIES

Lamb pairs well with fruits, and when matched up with the glorious fruits of summer, the results are dazzling. You're going to love this recipe, trust me.

*Elegant*
*Good for company*
*Kid-friendly*
*On a budget*
*Serves 4*

1/2 cup honey
1 teaspoon ground cardamom
1 teaspoon ground cinnamon
1/2 teaspoon ground ginger
1 teaspoon ground mace
1 tablespoon coarse salt
1 teaspoon ground black pepper
1/2 cup coarsely chopped dried apricots
1/2 cup pitted fresh cherries if in season; otherwise, dried will work
3 tablespoons butter
2 tablespoons lemon juice
1 butterflied half leg of lamb (For a whole butterflied leg, double the above ingredients.)

Heat a small saucepan over a medium flame. Add the butter, then sauté the apricots and cherries for 3-5 minutes. Stir in 1 tablespoon of the lemon juice and 1/4 cup honey. If the leg of lamb is netted, remove the netting and open the roast. Pour the fruit mixture inside, then tie the roast shut.

In a small saucepan, warm the remaining 1/4 cup honey over a gentle flame just until it is runny. Do not allow it to boil. Whisk in the remaining lemon juice, salt and spices. Rub the glaze into the outer surface of the roast. Allow the meat to come to room temperature while you prepare the grill.

If using a charcoal grill, build the fire, then rake the hot coals into 2 rows, each 4 inches from where the spit will turn. Place a drip pan in the center.

If working on a gas grill, preheat the front and rear burners on high. Set the drip pan over the center burner (if your rotisserie sits too close to the flame, you might have to set the drip pan underneath the grate).

Set your rotisserie attachment in place. Skewer the lamb on the spit and turn on the motor. Cover the grill and allow the meat to cook 1–1 1/2 hours, until an internal thermometer registers 120–145 degrees. Make sure the internal temperature of the cooking chamber stays around 350 degrees while the meat roasts. Allow the meat to rest 5–10 minutes before carving.

## HOW TO CARVE A WHOLE LEG OF LAMB

*It's all about flair.* When carving a whole, bone-in leg, some hosts feel compelled to first hack open the glistening, savory roast and saw out the bone. Not only does this generate a lot of unnecessary labor, frustration and manhandling of the meat, but it also creates an atmosphere of stress and anxiety for your diners, who are likely to hear you cursing under your breath as the knife threatens to make your fingers part of the menu.

Out of love and respect for yourself and your guests, the next time you host a leg of lamb dinner, make sure your carving knife is well-sharpened, then bring the entire leg, fresh from the grill or the oven, directly to the table for all to admire. Using a clean towel, grip the roast by the smaller shank end, lift it up slightly, then make long, wide slices down the length. Always be sure to end each slice with a dramatic flourish, much like a concert cellist would handle her bow. Done appropriately and with enough drama, guests will think little of the juices running down your front, and the occasionally slipping carving platter will only be material for the show. Most importantly, you will no longer have to wrestle with the roast as your guests look on in horror.

# LEMON-GARLIC LAMB KEBABS

While traveling through Spain, we feasted on lamb braised with lemon and garlic. We found this flavor pairing works equally well as a marinade for kebabs. This has become one of our favorite recipes. If you like, skewer up some fresh summer vegetables to grill alongside the meat.

Remember! Marinades impart *flavor,* not tenderness. Meats that are left in a high-acid marinade for too long will be mushy and gray, and much of the savory meat flavor will be lost.

*Minimal preparation*
*Kid-friendly*
*On a budget*
*Serves 4*

1/3 cup lemon juice
1/4 cup olive oil
1 small onion, finely chopped
4 cloves garlic, crushed
2 tablespoons paprika
1/4 cup fresh parsley, chopped
2 teaspoons coarse salt
2 teaspoons ground black pepper
1 fresh lemon, cut into wedges (optional)
2 pounds lamb kebabs
metal skewers, or bamboo skewers soaked 30
    minutes in water

Remove the lamb kebabs from the package and butterfly them by slicing almost through the center of each cube. This enables the marinade to penetrate the meat more deeply.

In a stainless-steel or other non-reactive bowl, whisk together the lemon juice, olive oil, onion, garlic, paprika, parsley, salt and pepper until a paste forms. Add the lamb and stir to coat. Cover and refrigerate 4 hours or overnight, stirring once or twice during the marinating period. Do *not* marinate longer than one day.

Light the grill and allow it to warm with the lid in place until the grate is hot. When it is fully warmed, you should be able to hold your hand 5 inches above the grate for no more than 2 or 3 seconds. Scrape the grate clean with a wire brush. Place the kebabs on skewers, then gently blot off any excess marinade with a paper towel. Lay the skewers directly over the flame. Cover the grill. Turn the skewers one-quarter turn every two minutes for medium-rare meat (for a total of 8 minutes cooking time). Serve the kebabs with the lemon wedges so your guests can add additional juice to taste.

## GAUGING MEAT TEMPERATURES ON THE ROTISSERIE.

Ok, maybe it's obvious...but I'll admit that I had to think about this for a few seconds when I first got my rotisserie. I'm always harping on the importance of using an internal meat thermometer, but if your roast is spinning around on a spit, the wires for the thermometer will get all tangled up. Using a rotisserie is one of those instances where timetables are definitely helpful. Based on the recipe, get an estimated time of when the meat should be done, then periodically stop the rotisserie just long enough to take the internal temperature and see how the meat is doing. When I get within ten degrees of my ideal temperature, I leave the motor of the rotisserie off, insert the thermometer, put the grill lid back in place (if appropriate), then let the meat sit still while it cooks the last few degrees. Until someone develops a remote, wire-free probe, that's the best I can do. The good news is that with a rotisserie and a carefully monitored cooking chamber, the grill temperatures will not be so hot as to easily over-cook your meat.

# SMOKED LAMB SHANKS WITH BLACK OLIVES

While the bacon and black olives might conjure images of cold-weather braising done indoors on the stove, try this recipe with classic Spanish flavors on your grill on a crisp fall day, where the smoke will add a layer of seasoning that could never be achieved in the kitchen.

*Good for company*
*On a budget*
*Serves 2–4*

4 tablespoons olive oil
4 slices thick-cut bacon, cut into strips
4 cloves garlic, minced
1/4 cup fresh oregano, finely chopped
1 quart chicken broth
1 fresh red chili pepper, seeds and white membrane removed, finely chopped (a dried chili pepper will work, too)
1/2 cup pitted black olives
1 tablespoon salt
1 tablespoon ground black pepper
2-4 pounds lamb shanks
several handfuls of hardwood chips or chunks, soaked in water (if using a charcoal grill)

Combine the salt and pepper on a plate, and roll the lamb shanks across, lightly coating them.

Light a large, hot fire in your grill. Set a deep cast-iron skillet over the flames and allow the skillet to warm. Add the olive oil, then add the shanks and bacon. Cook until the shanks are well-browned. Add the garlic and sauté 2-3 minutes, then add the oregano and chicken broth and stir well. If using a charcoal grill or gas grill with a smoke chamber, add a few wood chips or chunks to the fire or smoke chamber.

Place the lid down on the grill, making sure the vents (if using a charcoal grill) are open. Allow the meat to simmer for 30 minutes. Add the chopped red chili pepper and black olives, then simmer 30 minutes more, or until the shanks are fork-tender. If using charcoal, be sure to add more occasionally to maintain adequate heat.

Spoon the shanks, along with the broth, into shallow bowls. Serve with crusty bread and a green salad.

CHAPTER FOUR

# Pork

Every farmer needs four best friends: a border collie to move the livestock; a guard dog to protect them; a good barn cat for catching mice and rats, and a pig to handle the rest.

If there is any work on the land you are not willing to do yourself, chances are a pig will happily step in and give you aid. They will clean up all table scraps, making no fussy distinctions between meat, vegetables, or overly spicy foods. They will turn your compost (although watch out, because they have a tendency to eat more than their fair share of worms), clear brush, open up land, plow fields, even help construct ponds (and, as a point of fact, pigs happen to be decent swimmers). Pigs have been used for centuries in France to hunt out truffles. They will even help farmers find drafts in their barns when making repairs. At harvest, the generous pig provides: lard for salves, soap and baking; intestines for chitterlings (pronounced "chitlins" down south) and sausage casings; and a number of southern delicacies, like brains and eggs, hog jowl, blood pudding, pork rinds, head cheese, and pickled ears and feet. Even the skin and hair are useful. Then, of course, there are the numerous cuts of meat that even us less adventurous Yankees wax poetic about: juicy rib roasts and grilled pork chops, sausages of all kinds, bacons, hams, and most especially, barbecued ribs and pork shoulders. And even us

Yanks know what a treat it is to dive into a flaky biscuit or pie crust baked with lard.

In his tome to the pig, *The Complete Book of Pork,* Bruce Aidells reminds us that scholars are actually unsure about whether man domesticated pigs, or whether the clever creatures tamed themselves, realizing that humans offered protection and food. The relationship has lasted since about 10,000 B.C. (1) In Europe, pigs were principal nourishment for the Gauls, and the Romans feasted on them whole, reportedly boiling them on one side and roasting them on the other (perhaps they could have used a few lessons at a Southern BBQ pit). China, however, is the world's largest consumer of pork, where there is one pig for every three people (and there are *a lot* of people over there!)

There are many cultures that do not eat pork; in fact, about 20 percent of the world's population does not consume it. Apparently, ancient Israelites did consume pork prior to the Torah's injunction against it in Leviticus 11:7 (1). Some scholars suggest the prohibition came about because pigs were regarded as "unclean," since they would consume human waste, if permitted access, or because the meat would spoil easily, or perhaps—though not fully understood at the time—because of trichinosis infections.

Speaking of trichinosis, even today these pesky nematodes that live in the intestine and produce larvae that enter the muscle tissue of pigs keep too many people from enjoying pork in its full, juicy splendor. Fears of the disease lead many to assiduously adhere to the USDA's instructions to cook pork to a minimum of 160 degrees, resulting in pork chops and roasts that bear more resemblance to cardboard than to the luscious, savory, juicy bites of perfection that nature intended. Trichinae (which have not been found in this country for some time) are killed at 137 degrees, and pork will be succulent and delicious at a mere 145 degrees. Pastured pigs, in contrast with the modern, pink, ultra-lean factory pig, often contain older genetics in their bloodlines that enable them to thrive outdoors in natural conditions, away from confinement. The result is better marbled meat that will be more forgiving to work with. Over-cooking it slightly won't result in a ruined feast, as it would with factory-farmed pork. Still, going beyond 145 degrees puts you at risk for less-than-perfect pork. As meat cooks, the muscle fibers shrink; at 140 degrees, the fibers have contracted enough to begin squeezing moisture out of the cells. As the internal temperature climbs from 140 degrees to 160 degrees, the loss of moisture is accelerated, causing the meat to dry out and become tough (1). If you are cooking a hearty pastured pig with a fair amount of intramuscular fat, the melting of the fat will compensate for some of the water loss, creating a more pleasant mouth feel. But be forewarned: I regard any efforts to bring the internal temperature above 150 degrees to be an excessively reckless flirt with the flame, promising only disaster at the grill.

Finally, it is impossible to write about grilling and barbecuing pork without offering due respect to the Southern masters, the keepers of many of our nation's greatest food traditions. Hogs came to Jamestown with the first English settlers, although feral ones were already running free, thanks to earlier Spanish explorers. Thus, pork was central fare all through the South, regardless of race or class. Pork even played a role in the Civil Rights Movement when Ollie's Barbecue in Birmingham, Alabama, filed suit against the Justice Department following the Civil Rights Act of 1964, claiming that it should not be required to serve black restaurant patrons (2). Still, even today, the South reportedly consumes a full 25 percent of the United States' pork production (3). In the recipes that follow, whenever barbecue has been involved, I have been careful to adhere to the principles taught by Southern friends, although I occasionally borrow from a few other great pork cultures like Jamaica and China for added inspiration and innovation. I hope the legendary barbecue aficionados on the other side of the Mason-Dixon will exercise forbearance with my Yankee explanations and cross-cultural methodologies!

1. B. Aidells, *Bruce Aidells Complete Book of Pork*, HarperCollins, 2004.

2. John T. Edge, *Southern Belly: The Ultimate Food Lover's Companion to the South*, Hill Street Press, 2000.

3. J. S. Reed and D.V. Reed, *1001 Things Everyone Should Know About the South*, Broadway Books, 2002.

# COOKING SAUSAGES

Ever since we became licensed to process our own meat, we've gone link-happy at Sap Bush Hollow Farm. We now produce about twelve different varieties of sausages on the farm, ranging from chili-ale and chorizo, to beef mustard and bratwurst. We've spent a lot of hours blending, linking and grilling these wonders and, naturally, we have a few opinions about how good-quality artisan farm-fresh sausages should be handled.

*Don't pierce your sausages.* While factory-made sausages are often a mechanism for disposing of lower-quality meat and large volumes of fat, the opposite is true on the farm. Many farmers dedicate high-quality, meaty primals to the sausage cause, including the legs and shoulders of the pig. While typical grocery store sausages might contain 35–50 percent fat, very often farm sausages are about 20 percent fat, the same as a good quality hamburger (breakfast sausages, however, should have a slightly higher fat content). While all the fun spices are what characterize different sausage varieties, what makes these natural casing-wrapped bits of meat particularly special is the cooking process. When the meat and fats and spices are all wrapped up in a casing and exposed to heat, the fats melt and bubble and subsequently braise the meat and spices, creating the unique flavor. Those unfortunate fat-fearing folks who prick the links to drain them are really undermining all the wizardry that went into creating these little wonders. Furthermore, to add even more flair, many artisan sausage makers will add different liquids to their blends, such as beer, broth, or wine. Like the fats, these liquids serve to braise the meat in the casing. Pricking the skins of the sausages will only result in the loss of these tasty fluids, producing a dry, mealy sausage.

*Be gentle with your little links.* A typical *asado* in Argentina is often preceded first by a sausage course. Sweet links are removed from the grill and served plain in crusty bread, making a delightful sandwich called *chori-pan*. While the *costillas*, beef ribs, and *vacio*, large cuts of flank, would be slow-cooked for hours before the meal, I initially assumed that the sausages were tossed on at the last minute before everyone was ready to eat, as they typically are here in the U.S. Not so. Very often the sausages are first hung in the hearth a good distance from the flames and embers, where they warm slowly. Over the course of about 90 minutes, they are progressively moved closer to the intense heat, allowing the fats and liquids in the casing to slowly melt and bubble, braising the meat gently and giving the seasonings plenty of time to incorporate into the cooked meat. By the time the sausages are removed from the grill, the casings are crisp and taut with nary a burn mark, the meat is perfectly cooked and juicy, and not a single chorizo has burst. By contrast, in the United States I've seen many backyard grillers toss the links directly into the flames, allowing them to blacken or burst in the intense heat as the fats and fluids come to a rapid boil, all in the course of about 10–15 minutes. While it may not be necessary to cook your links for a full hour and a half, do consider moderating the flame and allowing the meat to come up to temperature by indirect cooking instead, cooking them gently for about 25–30 minutes. You'll likely find the meat tastier, juicier, and the casing much snappier.

# SALT AND PEPPER PORK CHOPS

Once again, the best way to taste your first pasture-raised pork chops is without all the frippery. I used to believe pork chops always required fancy herbal seasonings until one day I had grilled pork chops at the farm, cooked by my dad. I raved about the seasoning the entire evening and pleaded with Dad to tell me his recipe. He said nothing the whole night until I was walking out the door, at which point he called out, "salt and pepper!"

*Remember:* The most important consideration when grilling pork chops is to not over-cook them. Even if you are accustomed to well-done pork (yucky!), keep these chops on the rare side of medium, not letting the internal temperature rise above 145 degrees. This will keep the meat juicy and flavorful.

> *Elegant*
> *Good for company*
> *Minimal preparation*
> *Kid-friendly*
> *On a budget*
>
> **coarse salt, to taste**
> **fresh ground pepper, to taste**
> **pork chops, roughly 1 1/4-inch thick; figure on**
> **one pork chop per person**

Sprinkle the chops liberally with salt and pepper, then allow them to come to room temperature while you prepare the grill.

Heat one side of the grill to medium-high. You should be able to hold your hand five inches above the grate for no more than four seconds. Lay the chops directly over the flame and grill, with the lid off, for 1 1/2 minutes per side. Move the chops to the cool side of the grill and cook, covered, 10-12 minutes longer, without flipping, until the internal temperature of the meat registers between 137 and 145 degrees. Remove them to a platter, tent loosely with foil, and allow the meat to rest a few minutes before serving. This allows the juices to redistribute. The temperature of the meat will likely rise a few more degrees.

# GINGER LIME PORK CHOPS

Ok, you've successfully completed Pork Chops (101) by trying them with just salt and pepper. Now you've graduated to a fun variation...

*Elegant*
*Kid-friendly*
*On a budget*
*Serves 2 (to serve more, simply double or triple the*
*quantities in the marinade as needed)*

**1/4 cup lime juice**
**2 tablespoons fresh ginger, minced**
**2 tablespoons tamari**
**4 tablespoons peanut oil**
**3 tablespoons honey**
**2 large cloves garlic, minced**
**3 star anise, whole (optional)**
**2 pork chops, approximately 1 1/4-inch thick**

Whisk together the lime juice, ginger, tamari, peanut oil, honey, garlic and star anise. Set the pork chops in a shallow non-reactive bowl or pan (or zip-lock bag), then pour the mixture on top. Turn to coat. Marinate 1–2 hours, turning occasionally. When ready to grill, remove the meat and blot it dry. Allow the chops to come to room temperature while you prepare the grill.

Heat one side of the grill to medium-high. You should be able to hold your hand five inches above the grate for four seconds. Lay the chops directly over the flame and grill, with the lid off, for 1 1/2 minutes per side. Move the chops to the cool side of the grill and cook, covered, 10–12 minutes longer, without flipping, until the internal temperature of the meat registers between 137 and 145 degrees. Remove the chops to a platter and tent loosely with foil. Allow them to rest a few minutes before serving.

# GARLIC TERIYAKI PORK KEBABS

On the days when we process pork at the farm, the first thing the "cutting crew" does is seize the leg and bone out the ham and make a pile of several pounds of pork kebabs. We promptly carry a large portion of the kebabs inside to my parents, who use this marinade to make our lunch, and we all make real pigs of ourselves (ha).

*Good for company*
*Kid-friendly*
*On a budget*
*Serves 4*

1 cup frozen orange juice concentrate
6 cloves garlic, minced
1/2 cup soy sauce
1/3 cup honey
1/4 cup rice wine or sherry
4 tablespoons sesame oil
2 tablespoons fresh ginger, chopped
2–3 green peppers, cubed
1 cup pineapple, chunked
1 cup cherry tomatoes
2 onions, cut in wedges
2 pounds pork kebabs
metal skewers, or bamboo skewers soaked 30
    minutes or more in water

Remove the pork kebabs from the package and butterfly them by slicing almost through the center of each cube. This enables the marinade to more fully penetrate the meat.

In a stainless-steel or other non-reactive bowl, whisk together the orange juice concentrate, garlic, soy sauce, honey, wine, 2 tablespoons of the sesame oil and the ginger. Reserve 1/2 cup for glazing the vegetables, then add the pork to the remaining marinade. Stir to coat. Cover and refrigerate 4 hours or overnight, turning once or twice during the marinating period.

Do *not* marinate longer than a day, or the meat will become mushy.

Just before grilling, remove the meat from the marinade, spear it onto the skewers, then blot it dry. Spear the fruit and vegetables separately. Brush the vegetables with the reserved teriyaki marinade. Brush the kebabs with the remaining sesame oil. Allow everything to come to room temperature while you prepare the grill.

Light the grill and allow it to warm with the lid down until it is hot. When it is fully warmed, you should be able to hold your hand 5 inches above the grate for no more than 2–3 seconds. If you are cooking with charcoal, you might need to layer the coals a bit higher than usual in order to achieve this temperature.

Scrape the grate clean with a wire brush. Place all the skewers directly over the flame. Turn them one-quarter turn every 3 minutes, covering the grill between turns, until the meat is nicely browned. The total cooking time should be about 12 minutes. Serve the meat and vegetables with rice.

## WHO CHOOSES YOUR DINNER?

When my husband and I were first given our little Weber kettle, we thought it a lavish gift. With a price tag a little over $100, it had been a luxury beyond our limited means. Today, the price tag on a little charcoal kettle pales in comparison to the other options on the market. Ceramic charcoal grills can cost upwards of $800. Some grandiose outdoor gas grills can run several thousand dollars. The outdoor kitchen seems to be big money in this country right now.

But the indoor kitchen seems to be even bigger money. *Kitchen and Bath Business'* Market Forecaster report estimated that Americans would spend $68.3 billion remodeling their kitchens in 2005. Sadly, despite the money we put into them, Americans are apparently spending less and less time in the heart of the home. According to the USDA, in 1900 a typical woman spent 44 hours per week preparing meals and cleaning up after them. Today, the U.S. Energy Information Administration claims that over one in five households turns on its oven less often than once per week. Market research done by Kraft foods shows that, on average, American families spend less than 30 minutes eating dinner together, and that in 94 percent of American households, the children are choosing the weeknight menus. Interestingly, average American kids see 28 hours of television per week, about 20,000 commercials per year and, according to the A.C. Neilson company, kids' favorite television ads are for food products and fast-food restaurants. In short, our children are choosing what we eat, and their options

are laid out for them on the television screen.

It is true that organic foods are now claiming a piece of the market share in this country. However, increasingly, the same large food corporations that are bombarding your kids with TV ads, including Coca-Cola, M&M Mars, Pepsi, Tyson, Cargill, Kraft and General Mills (1) also own organic product lines, offering highly packaged, resource-intensive foods that are produced according to USDA's lax organic standards. These corporations are not foolish. They see organic food as a hot trend, but they also see that Americans, on the whole, are not willing to change the *way* they eat. Though we may care about the planet and prefer healthier foods, we still overwhelmingly value pre-packaged convenience. We are reluctant to actually spend time cooking fresh, wholesome food. Thus, while these corporate-owned prepared organic foods might be marginally healthier, in the end they don't benefit our local growers or communities, they continue to be shipped around the planet, they require excessive packaging, and they do nothing to improve our true quality of life.

What does all this mean? All of us in the sustainable cuisine movement believe that by changing what we eat in this country, we can make huge strides toward saving the planet. Eating local, organic, sustainably grown and pasture-raised foods reduces our reliance on fossil fuels. It cuts down on the chemicals that are dumped into the earth. It increases our food security, benefits our health, and improves our local economies. However, if we are not willing to change <u>how</u> we eat—that is, invest time cooking real, regional food in our kitchens—we will make very little progress in creating a vibrant local food economy. Rather, large food corporations will continue to dominate our dinner tables by way of our television screens, reaching out to our children and telling them what we should be eating.

If we really want to change the world, I suggest it's time to turn off that TV and bring our kids out to the farmers' market, into the kitchen, and out to the grill for some tasty lessons on global transformation.

1. P. Howard, *Organic Industry Structure*, Center for Agroecology and Sustainable Food Systems, University of California, Santa Cruz, 2005.

# Mediterranean Style Pork Kebabs

When working with pork kebabs, the seasoning possibilities are endless. I came up with this recipe after we tasted our way through Spain, Italy and Portugal.

*Good for company*
*On a budget*
*Serves 4*

1 small onion, minced
4 cloves garlic, minced
1/2 cup fresh parsley, chopped
2 tablespoons sweet paprika
1 teaspoon coriander
1/2 teaspoon ground cumin
1/4 teaspoon cayenne pepper
2 teaspoons salt
1 cup red wine
1/3 cup olive oil
2–3 green peppers, cubed
1 cup cherry tomatoes
2 onions, cut into wedges
2 pounds pork kebabs
metal skewers, or bamboo skewers soaked 30
    minutes or more in water

Remove the pork kebabs from the package and butterfly them by slicing almost through the center of each cube. This enables the marinade to more fully penetrate the meat.

In a stainless-steel or other non-reactive bowl, whisk together the minced onion, garlic, parsley, paprika, coriander, cumin, cayenne, salt, wine and olive oil. Reserve 1/2 cup for glazing the vegetables, then add the pork to the remaining marinade. Stir to coat. Cover and refrigerate 4 hours or overnight, turning once or twice during the marinating period. Do *not* marinate longer than a day, or the meat will become mushy.

Just before grilling, remove the meat from the marinade, spear it onto the skewers, then blot it dry. Spear the vegetables separately. Brush the vegetables with the reserved marinade. Allow everything to come to room temperature while you prepare the grill.

Light the grill and allow it to warm with the lid down until it is hot. When it is fully warmed, you should be able to hold your hand 5 inches above the grate for no more than 2–3 seconds. If you are cooking with charcoal, you might need to layer the coals a bit higher than usual in order to achieve this temperature.

Scrape the grate clean with a wire brush. Place all the skewers directly over the flame. Turn them one-quarter turn every 3 minutes, covering the grill between turns, until the meat is nicely browned. The total cooking time should be about 12 minutes.

# Rosemary Garlic Pork Roast

Here's another excuse to go get one of those rotisserie attachments I've been raving about. I've given instructions for preparing this roast using the indirect method, but really, the rotisserie version is better!

*Elegant*
*Good for company*
*Serves 6*

**4-6 cloves garlic**
**1/4 cup fresh rosemary, stemmed**
**2 tablespoons coarse salt**
**1 tablespoon ground black pepper**
**2 teaspoons ground mustard**
**1/3 cup olive oil**
**1 boneless fresh ham, loin or rib pork roast,**
**about 3 pounds**

Place the garlic, rosemary, salt, pepper, mustard and olive oil in a food processor and purée to make a paste. Rub the mixture into the meat, wrap it in plastic, then refrigerate for 2–4 hours. (Note: If you're short on time, you can skip the marinating period and get right to grilling.) Allow the meat to come to room temperature before grilling.

ROTISSERIE METHOD: If using a charcoal grill, build the fire, then rake the hot coals into 2 rows, each 4 inches from where the spit will turn. Cover the grill and allow it to warm to about 325 degrees. Place a drip pan in the center.

If using a gas grill, preheat the front and rear burners on high until the cooking chamber is 325 degrees. Set the drip pan over the center burner.

Put your rotisserie attachment in place. Skewer the roast on the spit and turn on the motor. Cover the grill and allow the meat to roast approximately 20-22 minutes per pound, maintaining the cooking chamber between 300 and 350 degrees. Remove the meat from the spit once the internal temperature is between 140 and 150 degrees. Tent loosely with foil and allow the meat to rest 10 minutes before carving. The internal temperature will rise another 5-10 degrees during this time.

INDIRECT METHOD: Light one side of the grill and put the lid in place. Allow the cooking chamber to come up to 325 degrees. Scrape the grill clean. Set a drip pan below where the meat will sit on the cool side of the grate. Lay the roast on the grill above the drip pan. (Alternatively, put the roast in a cast-iron skillet, but still place it on the cool side of the grill.) Close the grill. If using charcoal, turn the lid so the vents are open over the meat. Monitor the grill temperature, ensuring that it stays between 300 and 350 degrees. Add additional coals, or adjust the vents and dials as necessary. Allow the meat to cook for roughly 20-22 minutes per pound, or until an internal meat thermometer registers 140-150 degrees. Remove the meat from the grill and tent loosely with foil while it rests for 10 minutes. The internal temperature will rise another 5-10 degrees during this time.

# CHILI CHOCOLATE PORK RIBS

Cinnamon and cocoa add a touch of exotic bitterness to this otherwise classic dish. If the departure from tradition makes you nervous, use the Paprika-Pepper Spice Rub on page 129, or the Maple-Ginger Spice Rub on page 120.

When buying ribs, figure on 1 pound of spare ribs per person, or one country rib per person.

*Good for company*
*Kid-friendly*
*On a budget*
*Serves 2-4*

2 tablespoons paprika
2 tablespoons unsweetened cocoa
2 tablespoons chili powder
4 teaspoons coarse salt
1 tablespoon ground black pepper
1 tablespoon ground cinnamon
1/4 cup sucanat, turbinado or other unrefined or
    partially refined sugar
barbecue sauce (use either Maple-Bourbon Glaze,
    p. 121, Southern-Style Butter Barbecue Sauce,
    p. 130, Sweet Tomato Barbecue Sauce, p. 62, or
    a good-quality bottled sauce)
pork spare ribs or country ribs, 2–4 pounds
several handfuls of hickory, apple or mesquite
    chips or chunks, soaked in water for a mini-
    mum of 30 minutes (If you are using a gas
    grill, only use wood chips, in which case you
    will need about 2 cups.)

The night before you plan to barbecue, thoroughly combine the paprika, cocoa, chili powder, salt, pepper, cinnamon and sugar in a shallow bowl. Apply the rub evenly over the ribs by sprinkling generously and massaging it in. Reserve any extra for another use by storing it in an airtight container (note: be sure that you have not handled the reserved spice with hands that have handled raw meat). Wrap the meat in plastic and refrigerate.

On BBQ day, remove the meat from the refrigerator, unwrap it and allow it to come to room temperature. If using a gas BBQ, light the grill, then put the soaked wood chips in a foil tray and set it down directly over one burner. Close the lid and preheat the grill on high until the smoke billows out. Turn off all but the one burner beneath the wood chips, and allow the temperature to come down to about 200 to 230 degrees. If the chamber won't cool down that low, get it as low as you can, then plan for a shorter cook time.

If using charcoal, start the grill and warm it until the temperature inside the cooking chamber is between 200 and 230 degrees. Toss a handful of soaked wood chips or chunks directly over the coals.

Lay the meat, bone-side down, on the cool side of the grate and set the cover in place. If using a charcoal grill, open the vents partially and arrange them so they are directly over the meat.

Smoke the ribs (do not flip them!) roughly 1 hour and 15 minutes per pound, adding coals and additional wood chips or chunks as necessary for the charcoal grill or adjusting the dial as needed on the gas grill. The temperature of the cooking chamber should always be between 200 and 230 degrees.

After one hour, brush the ribs down with the barbecue sauce. When the meat is tender and the tissue around the ribs has pulled away from the bone, supper is served. Cut the ribs apart and serve with additional barbecue sauce.

# Smoked Country Ribs, Jerk Style

There are as many sensual pleasures in preparing this recipe as there are in eating it. The colors and smells of the different spice combinations, the feel of the paste on the meat, and the heat of the grill build up to a great feast. Have fun with this one.

*Good for company*
*On a budget*
*Serves 6*

**Coffee-Allspice Jerk Paste (p. 116)**
**Tamarind-Ginger Barbecue Sauce (p. 117)**
**6 country-style ribs**
**several handfuls of hickory or mesquite chips or**
**chunks, soaked in water for a minimum of 30**
**minutes (If you are using a gas grill, only use**
**wood chips, and you will need about 2 cups.)**

The night before you plan to barbecue, thoroughly coat the country ribs in the Coffee-Allspice Jerk Paste. Wrap the meat in plastic and refrigerate.

On BBQ day, remove the meat from the refrigerator, unwrap it and allow it to come to room temperature. If using a gas BBQ, light the grill, then put the soaked wood chips in a foil tray and set it down directly over one burner. Close the lid and preheat the grill on high until the smoke billows out. Turn off all but the one burner beneath the wood chips, and allow the temperature to come down to about 200 to 230 degrees. If the chamber won't cool down that low, get it as low as you can, then plan for a shorter cook time.

If using charcoal, start the grill and warm it until the temperature inside the cooking chamber is around 230 degrees. Toss a handful of soaked wood chips or chunks directly over the coals.

Lay the meat on the cool side of the grate and set the grill cover in place. If using a charcoal grill, open the vents partially and arrange them so they are directly over the meat.

Smoke the ribs (do not flip them!) for about 4–5 hours, adding coals and additional wood chips or chunks as necessary for the charcoal grill or adjusting the dial as needed on the gas grill. The temperature of the cooking chamber should always be between 225 and 250 degrees. When the meat is cooked, it will be well-done, but tender and juicy. Brush the ribs with the Tamarind-Ginger Barbecue Sauce, then allow them to cook 10 minutes longer before serving.

# COFFEE-ALLSPICE JERK PASTE

**1/2 cup fresh parsley, chopped**
**3 tablespoons chives, minced**
**2 tablespoons dried onion flakes**
**1 teaspoon dried mustard**
**1 tablespoon ground cinnamon**
**2–3 teaspoons cayenne pepper**
**2 tablespoons ground allspice**
**2 tablespoons dried thyme**
**2 cloves garlic**
**1/4 cup lime juice (lemon juice can be substituted)**
**1/4 cup olive oil**
**1/4 cup honey**

Combine all the above ingredients in a food processor and blend to make a paste. Be sure to reserve 1/4 cup of the paste for the Tamarind-Ginger Barbecue Sauce.

# Tamarind-Ginger Barbecue Sauce

**2 cups chicken broth**
**1/2 cup honey**
**1 tablespoon dried ginger**
**1/4 cup Coffee-Allspice Jerk Paste (p. 116)**
**1 tablespoon tamarind paste***

Combine all the above ingredients in a saucepan. Bring the mixture to a boil, then reduce the heat and allow the sauce to simmer until it is reduced by one-third. Serve warm.

*\*Tamarind paste, made from the tamarind fruit, should be available in most well-stocked grocery stores. It is also available in many ethnic food markets. If you can't find it, make a substitute paste by puréeing equal parts chopped dates and dried apricots with lemon juice (1:1:1).*

# Maple-Bourbon Barbecued Ham

A fresh, uncured ham is a spectacular cut of meat. It is relatively inexpensive and, when left whole, it presents a glorious feast for a crowd. If you are so lucky as to procure a ham with the skin on (a rare find), you're in for an extra treat: cracklings, the crispy, crunchy bits of roasted fatty skin. The flavors in this recipe are so autumnal that when we tested this, we had a farewell-to-summer dinner party out on our porch, pairing it with the last of the season's sweet corn and the first of the season's winter squash.

When you make this, be sure to remove the ham from the freezer several days ahead so that it can thaw in your refrigerator. Also, the ham tastes best if it is allowed to soak up the dry rub for at least 24 hours before cooking. When feast day arrives, rise early, start up the barbecue, and enjoy a full, languid day tending to the slow fire while you taunt your neighbors with the great scents. If you're using charcoal, make sure you have a full bag on hand. If you're using gas, be sure your tank is full.

*Elegant feast*
*Good for company*
*Kid-friendly*
*On a budget*
*Serves 9-14, depending on the size of the roast*
*(allow 1 pound per person)*

**Maple-Ginger Spice Rub (p. 120)**
**Maple-Bourbon Glaze (p. 121)**
**1 fresh ham, 9-14 pounds**
**several handfuls of hickory or apple chips or chunks, soaked in water or apple cider for a minimum of 30 minutes (If you are using a gas grill, only use wood chips, and you will need about 2 cups.)**

One or two days before the feast, thoroughly massage the Maple-Ginger Spice Rub into the meat. If the skin has been left on, make several 1-inch gashes by piercing it with a stiff knife, and push the rub beneath the skin, down through the fat and into the meat (there is no need to dress the skin itself, as the rub will come off quickly). If there is no skin on the roast, massage the rub into the outer layer of fat, as well as into any exposed meat portions. Wrap in plastic and refrigerate overnight or for two days.

When you are ready to cook (*several hours* before serving time), unwrap the roast and allow it to come to room temperature. If using charcoal, start the grill and warm it until the temperature inside the cooking chamber is about 220 degrees F. If using a gas grill, light the grill, turn all burners to high, then put the 2 cups soaked wood chips in a foil tray and set it down directly over one burner. Close the lid and preheat the cooking chamber (all burners still on high) until smoke billows out. Turn off all but the one burner beneath the wood chips and allow the cooking chamber to come down to 200–230 degrees (if the chamber won't cool down that low, get it as cool as you can, then plan for a shorter cook time).

Place the ham in a large cast-iron skillet (or disposable roasting pan) on the side opposite the fire. If you are cooking with charcoal, toss some soaked wood chips or chunks on the embers. Close the grill lid. If you are using a charcoal grill, arrange the lid so that the vents are partially open and on the same side as the meat in order to draw the smoke through. Monitor the temperature of the smoking chamber throughout the day, making sure it stays between 170 and 230 degrees F. Add coals or adjust the flame as necessary. If cooking with charcoal, be sure to add more soaked wood chips or chunks each hour.

Cook the ham until the internal temperature is between 145–165 degrees F. Total cooking time will be roughly 30–40 minutes per pound of meat.

About 30 minutes before you remove the meat from the barbecue, bring the Maple-Bourbon Glaze to a simmer and use 1/3 of it to generously coat the meat. Once you've removed the roast, brush on the glaze once more, then allow the roast to rest 15-20 minutes before carving. To serve, reheat the remaining glaze to a simmer, then pass it separately with the carved pork.

# Maple-Ginger Spice Rub

1/2 cup granulated maple sugar (if this is not
   available near you, use sucanat or another
   unrefined sugar from a local health food
   store)
1/4 cup dried mustard
2 tablespoons cinnamon
1 tablespoon ground ginger
2 teaspoons cayenne pepper
1/2 cup coarse sea salt
1/4 cup ground black pepper
1/4 cup rubbed sage

Add all the above ingredients to a small bowl and mix well.

# Maple-Bourbon Glaze

**1/2 cup maple syrup**
**1/2 cup bourbon**
**1/2 cup cider vinegar**
**1/2 cup apple butter**
**1/4 cup Dijon mustard**
**1/3 cup apple cider**
**1 onion, finely chopped**
**1/2 cup butter**

To make the glaze, melt the butter in a sauce pan over medium heat. Add the finely chopped onion and sauté until translucent. Whisk in the remaining ingredients and allow the mixture to come to a boil for 30 seconds before reducing it to a simmer. Simmer for 30 minutes to thicken, then set aside.

When my daughter was ten months old, one of her favorite games was calling out the sounds of different animals from the farm. The sheep say "baa," the cows say "moo," etcetera. Throughout that spring we'd hike around the farm practicing our animal calls: "Woof!" "Meow!" "Whoop Whoop!" (That's a goose.) But for her, the game didn't stop in the barnyard. I'll never forget the Saturday night when I brought our weekly roasted chicken to the table and she looked up from her high chair and called out "Bawk! Bawk!" while she reached for the platter in a mad scramble for the drumstick.

She was a one-year-old when we packed off to France to study the food scene. One afternoon while traveling on the train, her daddy set about amusing her by drawing a critter on a piece of paper, and Saoirse, now with a more developed vocabulary, would call out the name. Daddy drew a picture of a dog. "Doggie!" she exclaimed. He drew a picture of a cat. "Kitty!" Then, he drew a picture of a chicken. She paused and stared at the drawing, then called out "Dinner!"

My children are growing up on a farm in a family that loves to cook. When selling meat at our markets, I have seen parents cover their children's ears when they ask us questions about our slaughter practices and our harvest schedules. They want to protect their children from the "hard truth" that animals are alive before they are dead and wrapped in plastic or butcher paper.

Life and death are too much a part of my family's daily existence for us to shelter our children from it. Saoirse sees her mommy and her friends at work in the slaughterhouse, cutting and wrapping lamb carcasses. She plays outside on chicken-processing days and has full awareness of the harvest process. In the kitchen she mixes the spice rubs after I measure them, then helps to season the meat. She stands beside me at the grill as I turn steaks and study their doneness. She knows when I'm testing meat recipes and lends her critiques. "Mommy, this is salty!" "Mommy, this is spicy!" Or finally, "Good recipe, Mommy!"

It is impractical, if not impossible, to hide the realities of farm life from her. Moreover, I think concealing the truth about slaughter is a disservice. In order to fully know about meat, we need to know something of the animal's life and, yes, its death.

So that we can prepare meat properly and enjoy it fully, we need to understand where the different cuts of meat come from on the animal. I meet a lot of customers who don't know that the tenderloin is tender because it comes from the part of the animal that does the least amount of work, or that chuck steaks are chewy because they come from the part of the animal that works most. In fact, a large number of people I meet couldn't tell a chuck roast from a rib roast, or a pork chop from a beef top loin steak!

My guess is that, 50 years ago, this was commonplace knowledge. However, as a nation we've stopped teaching our younger generations how to cook, and no longer relay any true understanding of where our food comes from. It wasn't always this way. In her 1940s-era book, *Let's Cook It Right*, Adelle Davis taught about the different cuts of meat by instructing greenhorn housewives to crawl around on the floor and explore how their different muscles were moving. Those muscles that worked hard were likely to be the cuts of meat that would require braising or pot roasting; those muscles that hardly moved could be pan-fried or quickly grilled.

However, sadly, somewhere in our country's unique cultural history, Americans have learned to disassociate the food on their tables with the animal that produced it. We have a tendency to vision chicken breasts without visioning the chicken, ham without picturing the rump of a pig. Our industrialized food system has neatly removed the notion of slaughter from view of the people who consume meat. The cuts of meat that end up in the butchers' section of the grocery store bear no resemblance to the animals from which they came. There is no discussion about what these animals were fed, how they were treated, or where they came from (until there's a mass recall of tainted meat). In fact, a person could, theoretically, go to the store and buy meat with no genuine awareness that it came from an animal.

The industrialization of food production and marketing has thoroughly discouraged us from linking the life and death of another living creature with our own. And by being so disconnected from our food, by passively disregarding the way animals are raised and slaughtered, we have inadvertently condoned the nation's large-scale livestock industry's use of unsanitary, inhumane, unnatural and ecologically destructive practices.

To be better cooks, to be at home in the kitchen and at the grill with grassfed meat, to ensure that we have a safe, healthful and sustainable food supply, we *must* have an awareness that our meat comes from living animals. To prepare meats properly, we need to have an understanding of the living animal, not just its separate parts. And we need to understand that honoring an animal's life through excellent care, and honoring its death through humane slaughter, is the way to honor our own lives with nourishing food.

# HONEY MANDARIN
# PORK SHOULDER

Chinese roasted pork, *char su*, is sticky sweet on the outside and succulent, moist and tender on the inside. Combine Chinese seasonings with the Southern-style method for making pulled pork, and you have a darn good meal.

*Good for company*
*Kid-friendly*
*On a budget*
*Serves 3–10*

**Chinese Marinade (p. 126)**
**Honey Mandarin Glaze (p. 126)**
**1 pork shoulder roast, Boston butt or picnic ham,**
    **3-10 pounds**
**several handfuls of hickory or apple chips or**
    **chunks, soaked in water for a minimum of 30**
    **minutes (If you are using a gas grill, only use**
    **wood chips, and you will need about 2 cups.)**

Place the pork shoulder in a large stainless-steel or other nonreactive bowl. Pour the Chinese Marinade on top, turn to coat, then cover and refrigerate 1–2 days.

On barbecue day, remove the meat, blot it dry, and allow it to come to room temperature while you prepare the grill.

If using charcoal, start the grill and warm it until the temperature inside the cooking chamber is about 220 degrees F. If using a gas grill, light the grill, turn all burners to high, then put the 2 cups soaked wood chips in a foil tray and set it down directly over one burner. Close the lid and preheat the cooking chamber (all burners still on high) until smoke billows out. Turn off all but the one burner beneath the wood chips and allow the cooking chamber to come down to 200–230 degrees (if the chamber won't cool down that low, get it as cool as you can, then plan for a shorter cook time).

Set a drip pan in place on the cool side of the grill. Lay the pork shoulder on top. If possible, arrange the meat so that the fat cap is facing up. If the roast is too tall, or if it won't balance with the fat cap on top, lay the meat on its side and arrange it so the fat cap faces the heat. This insulation will help protect the meat from drying out or over-cooking. If using a charcoal grill, toss some soaked wood chips or chunks directly on the coals. Put the lid in place. Open the vents of the lid partially and arrange them so they are directly over the meat. If using gas, simply close the lid.

Smoke the meat for roughly 1 hour and 15 minutes to 1 hour and 30 minutes per pound, adding coals as necessary (or adjusting the dial on your gas grill) to make sure the temperature of the cooking chamber stays between 200 and 230 degrees. Each time you add coals, brush the meat down with the Honey Mandarin Glaze and add a few more wood chips or chunks to the fire. If using gas, baste with the glaze once per hour. When the meat is fork-tender with an internal temperature around 185–200 degrees, it is ready. Remove it from the grill and allow it to rest 10–15 minutes before pulling it apart. Serve the meat with the remaining glaze on the side.

# CHINESE MARINADE

2 ribs celery, finely chopped
2 carrots, finely chopped
1 large onion, finely chopped
2 tablespoons minced fresh ginger
2 cloves garlic, minced
1/2 cup soy sauce
1 cup sake or sherry
3 tablespoons Hoisin sauce
1 tablespoon dry mustard
1/4 cup honey
6 star anise (optional)
2 tablespoons orange zest
2 tablespoons toasted sesame oil
1 cup frozen orange juice concentrate, thawed

Whisk together all the above ingredients in a large stainless-steel or non-reactive bowl.


# HONEY MANDARIN GLAZE

1/2 cup honey
1/2 cup frozen orange juice concentrate, thawed
2 tablespoons dark brown sugar
2-3 tablespoons salt

Whisk together all the above ingredients in a small sauce pan. Bring to a boil, then immediately turn off the heat, whisking gently as the mixture cools.

# CAROLINA-STYLE PULLED PORK

No grilling and barbecue book would be complete without paying homage to at least a few of those Southern pit masters who have elevated the union of pork and smoke to a high art.

*Good for company*
*Kid-friendly*
*On a budget*
*Serves 4–10*

1 batch Paprika-Pepper Spice Rub, p. 129
1 batch Vinegar Mop, p. 129
1 batch Southern-Style Butter Barbecue Sauce,
    p. 130
OPTIONAL: 1 can beer, or 2 cups apple cider
one pork shoulder roast, 4–10 pounds, either
    Boston butt or picnic roast will work
several handfuls of hickory chips or chunks,
    soaked in water for a minimum of 30 minutes
    (If you are using a gas grill, only use wood
    chips, and you will only need about 2 cups.)
    Note: As an option, our good friend and bar-
    becue aficionado, Frank Davis, suggests soak-
    ing the smoking wood in apple cider or beer
    for extra flavor.

Thoroughly coat the pork shoulder in the spice rub, reserving any extras for the vinegar mop. Wrap the meat in plastic and refrigerate for 1–2 days.

On barbecue day, remove the meat, unwrap it and allow it to come to room temperature.

If using charcoal, start the grill and warm it until the temperature inside the cooking chamber is about 220 degrees F. If using a gas grill, light the grill, turn all burners to high, then put the 2 cups soaked wood chips in a foil tray and set it down directly over one burner. Close the lid and preheat the cooking chamber (all burners still on high) until smoke billows out. Turn off all but the one burner beneath the wood chips and allow the cooking chamber to come down to 200–230 degrees (if the chamber won't cool down that low, get it as cool as you can, then plan for a shorter cook time).

Set a drip pan in place on the cool side of the grill. If you like, pour a can of beer or 2 cups apple cider into the pan to add additional moisture and flavor to the smoke process (this is optional, as the meat will smoke just fine without it). Lay the pork shoulder on top. If possible, arrange the meat so that the fat cap is facing up. If the roast is too tall, or if it won't balance with the fat cap on top, lay the meat on its side and arrange it so the fat cap faces the heat. This will help protect the meat from drying out or over-cooking. If using a charcoal grill, toss some soaked wood chips or chunks directly on the coals. Put the lid in place. Open the vents of the lid partially and arrange them so they are directly over the meat. If using gas, simply close the lid.

Smoke the meat for roughly 1 hour and 15 minutes to 1 hour and 30 minutes per pound, adding coals as necessary (or adjusting the dial on your gas grill) to make sure the temperature of the cooking chamber stays between 200 and 230 degrees. Each time you add coals, brush the meat down with the Vinegar Mop and add a few more wood chips or chunks to the fire. If using gas, baste with the mop once per hour. When the meat is fork-tender with an internal temperature around 185–200 degrees, it is ready. Remove the meat from the grill and allow it to rest 10–15 minutes before pulling it apart. Pass the meat with the barbecue sauce, allowing guests to pour it on themselves. Serve with Barbecue Slaw (page 131) and, if you like, hamburger buns.

## PULLED PORK SHORT CUT

Not enough time in your day to stand around monitoring the grill, waiting for pulled pork or the Honey Mandarin Pork Shoulder? No problem. Just smoke the meat 2–3 hours on your grill, then put the roast in a covered, non-reactive roasting pan, pour on some more sauce or glaze, set the lid in place and finish it in the oven at 300 degrees for a few hours until it is pull-apart tender.

# PAPRIKA-PEPPER SPICE RUB

1/3 cup ground black pepper
1/4 cup coarse salt
1/3 cup sucanat, turbinado or an unrefined or par-
    tially refined sugar
2 tablespoons dry mustard
1/3 cup mild paprika
1 tablespoon granulated garlic
1 tablespoon onion powder
1 teaspoon celery powder

Combine all the ingredients in a small bowl. Mix well.

# VINEGAR MOP

remaining paprika pepper rub left over after sea-
    soning the meat
3 cups cider vinegar
1 small onion, minced
2 tablespoons honey
2 teaspoons coarse salt
1 teaspoon ground black pepper
2 cloves garlic, minced
1-2 teaspoons cayenne pepper (optional)
1/4 cup ketchup

Combine all the ingredients in a medium-sized bowl and whisk
well.

# SOUTHERN-STYLE BUTTER BARBECUE SAUCE

This is an old-style, thin, vinegar-based sauce. If, after you taste it, you would prefer something a little thicker and sweeter, whisk in an additional 2 tablespoons Dijon or whole grain mustard and 1/4 cup molasses.

>  **8 tablespoons butter**
>  **1 medium onion, finely minced**
>  **3/4 cup cider vinegar**
>  **1 teaspoon ground black pepper**
>  **2 tablespoons Worcestershire sauce**
>  **2 tablespoons molasses**
>  **2 teaspoons dry mustard**
>  **salt to taste**

Melt the butter in a saucepan over medium heat. Add the onion and sauté until translucent, about 5 minutes. Whisk in the remaining ingredients and bring to a boil, then reduce the heat and simmer 5 minutes. Salt to taste. Serve warm.

# Barbecue Slaw

Enough with the cutesy shreds of apple or caraway seeds wrecking a perfectly good slaw. This is the only way to accompany good barbecued pork.

**1 head green cabbage, finely shredded**
**4 medium-sized carrots, finely shredded**
**1 cup mayonnaise**
**1 tablespoon chili powder**
**1 tablespoon paprika**
**2 teaspoons salt**
**2 teaspoons ground black pepper**
**1 teaspoon sucanat, turbinado or another unre-**
**  fined or partially refined sugar**
**2 tablespoons cider vinegar**
**2 tablespoons good barbecue sauce**

In a small bowl, mix together the chili powder, paprika, salt, pepper and sugar.  In a large bowl, combine the cabbage and carrots. Stir in the mayonnaise, chili powder, paprika, salt, pepper, sugar, vinegar and barbecue sauce. If there's time, cover the bowl and allow it to rest in the refrigerator for a few hours before serving. If you're too hungry to wait, just dig in.

# IS BARBECUING REALLY A GUY THING?

For weeks we haunted Caseros, the noisy, run-down outskirts of Buenos Aires. Migrants from the rural north, Nestor Gomez and his wife Graciela had turned their tiny patch of land into a tropical paradise framed by blossoming bougainvillea, jasmine, roses, lemon verbena and citrus trees, creating a world apart from the trash-littered streets just outside their garden walls. It was in this garden, while the scent of jasmine hung heavy in the air, where I sat in the *quincho*, the outdoor kitchen, and studied Nestor's every movement around the fire and embers of the *parilla*. I learned to test the flames with my hands, to study the glow of the embers and to watch the meat closely, studying how it sweated, contracted, and pulled away from the bones. For weeks I shadowed this *asador*, mimicking his every movement, longing for a chance to cook an *asado* myself, to tango with the embers like Nestor.

My teacher was diligent in his explanations about controlling the fire, about meat science and flavoring principles. We kept a notebook and paper out by the open hearth, and he'd draw diagrams of the different cooking traditions he'd seen in South America. But he was reluctant to surrender his grill to me. "*Hacer el asado es cosa de hombres,*" he quipped when I first asked for a solo night in the *quincho*. *Grilling is a man's thing.* Free from presumptive notions about a man's and woman's rightful place, Nestor couldn't resist teasing me with the oft-repeated macho phrase about the Argentine grill scene.

But many a truth is said in jest. And as we traveled around the country from one *parilla* to the next, the men presided over the fires.

And it isn't just in Argentina where men rule the flames. Here, too, in the United States, grills are the classic Father's Day gift, cookouts are the man's domain, and I've met few women who actually know how to light their backyard barbecues.

Despite my XX chromosomes, I felt drawn to the intense heat pouring out of the outdoor hearth; I was attracted to those flames; I wanted to shovel the embers and watch, touch, coax and smell the meat as it transformed from flesh to feast. Thus, as a final exam, at the end of my stay, Nestor transferred the rake, shovel, wood and embers to my care, grabbed a bottle of wine and took a seat on the patio while I prepared dinner. The air around the fire had to be over 100 degrees. My body dripped with sweat as I shoveled the coals and tested the heat. When the meat was finally cooked, I slipped out to the patio to join my dinner companions, who were deeply immersed in drink, music and conversation. I sat beside Graciela and across from her daughter, Sonia, and her daughter-in-law, Laura.

"*¿Como andas?*" How's it going? Graciela asked sympathetically, as she offered me a glass of iced lemon juice and Gancia, an unusual treat I'd learned to enjoy in Argentina's intense heat.

Great—I had relished every minute in the sweat lodge! They nodded politely as I spoke. I asked, "*¿No quieren* *hacerlo?" Don't you want to do it?* I couldn't understand why they never craved a chance to reign over the *quincho.*

"*¿Hacer asado?"* Graciela asked me incredulously. I nodded.

"*No,"* the three of them replied in unison.

Laura laughed. *"Hacer asado es el cosa des hombres,"* she reminded me.

She poured herself another glass of lemonade. Graciela refilled her iced wine. Sonia propped her feet on the chair beside her, then asked if I needed a towel to mop my sweaty forehead.

"Every day we prepare lunch," Sonia switched to English. "Every day we cook dinner. Why would we want to do the *asado?* It's our only night off!"

CHAPTER FIVE

# Poultry

I think chicken has been the one meat most roundly abused on backyard grills across North America. Sadly, we have an enduring tradition of buying the birds cut in parts, singeing the legs, thighs and breasts to the point of despair over flames, then drowning the dried-out meat in store-bought barbecue sauce, which is essentially high-fructose corn syrup dyed orange. Yuck. Carrying this image of "barbecued chicken," for years I found polite excuses to decline invitations to cookouts where chicken was the featured menu item, and I *never* approached my grill with one of our pristine pastured birds...until I had to write this book. Now I love chicken off the grill, provided it's done properly—not over-cooked or over-smoked and ideally, grilled whole.

One of the problems we typically face in North America when cooking poultry—be it in the kitchen or on the grill—is that we tend to over-cook it "to be safe." While salmonella bacteria is a legitimate concern when working with poultry, the bacteria is killed at 140 degrees. Thus, for chicken to be safely cooked, we don't need to incinerate it until the internal temperature reads 180 degrees, as many people believe. I find that an internal temperature of 165 degrees when working with clean, farm-raised pastured chickens is ideal.

Next, grilled chicken tastes great because gentle smoke from a well-managed fire lends an exciting flavor. I say *gentle* smoke, because it is easy to over-smoke this delicate meat and cover up the lovely natural flavor and texture that pastured chicken offers. After placing a chicken several hours in the smoker, very often the only thing I can taste is hickory or mesquite, and not the meat.

And finally, consider grilling your birds whole. At our farmers' market, many customers intent on grilling insist on buying cut-up birds. However, unless you are in a dire hurry, I think whole birds are easier to cook, the results are much better, and whole birds are cheaper than parts. Better still, the meat stays juicier and the slower cooking time results in a more flavorful meal. If your dinner companions are few and you can't eat the entire chicken, then the smoke-infused leftovers make heavenly chicken salads. In fact, I prefer chicken salads made from grilled birds, which is why I have included a number of these recipes in the following pages.

I've tried numerous methods for cooking whole chickens on the grill—butterflying, beer cans, indirect grill-roasting, and the rotisserie. While each of the following recipes features one of these methods, I have found that, for the most part, the methods are interchangeable.

Butterflying helps the bird to cook faster, but usually the same seasonings can be applied, with similar results achieved, on the spit, over the beer can, or using the indirect method. Simply allow for more cooking time if the bird is whole and not split open.

Beer cans are always the same size, but pastured chickens are not, and the birds will not always fit perfectly for the beer-can technique. I learned this the hard way when I tested the Poussin à la Moutarde on page 143 with a beer can and a five-and-a-half-pound chicken. I ruined a favorite shirt by imprinting it with a giant mustard-slathered bird when it slid off the can and against my chest as I carried it to the grill. My darkening mood was topped off when I placed the fowl on the grill and attempted to close the lid, only to have the darn thing flop over again, knocking off the rest of the sauce and spilling the beer all over the grate, inside the cavity of the bird and dousing the coals. I promptly re-seasoned the bird, then ran an experiment, cooking one using a beer can, and one using the indirect method. I found no significant difference, although the beer does lightly infuse the meat. The beer can holds the bird upright, enabling all sides of the bird to crisp beautifully, whereas the indirect method will leave the back side soggy (since I use the backs for soup stock, I'm not concerned about this).

After learning the beer can and indirect methods, I read a 1964 text, *La Cuisine de France*, by Mapie, La Countess de Toulouse-Lautrec, who devoted an entire book to the noble cause of helping Americans understand the great tradition of French cooking. There, she reveals that the best way to cook a chicken is on a spit. I gave that method a try. She was absolutely right. The rotisserie provides an even cook, the bird bastes in its own juices as it turns, and the skin crisps perfectly all the way around. If done over charwood, the smoke will perfume the meat without overpowering it, and dinner will be magnificent. Done on a gas grill, the rotisserie makes grilling the chicken as easy as roasting it whole in the oven, requiring very little attention until it is time to start checking the internal temperature of the meat. The rotisserie is also a great way to cook small and medium-sized Thanksgiving turkeys, as well as goose, duck and rabbit.

And speaking of which…rabbit is an excellent meat on the grill. I have not included any recipes specifically for rabbit, however; its taste and texture are somewhat similar to chicken, so rabbit and chicken recipes are usually interchangeable. So feel free to substitute rabbit for the chicken in the Poussin à la Moutarde, or to try a rotisseried lemon-roasted rabbit.

# Parsley Roasted Beer Can Chicken

We've all heard about the miracles of cooking a chicken on the grill by propping it over a beer can, but we may not have understood how it is done. Here, you finally have an explanation, with a recipe that uses gentle seasonings so that you can appreciate the smoky flavor that will infuse the chicken. The best part is that this recipe has you keep the bird in a cast-iron skillet, which captures all the luscious juices for pouring over the meat when you serve it. If you have a rotisserie, I've given instructions for that, as well.

*Minimal preparation*
*Kid-friendly*
*On a budget*
*Serves 4*

**1/4 cup olive oil**
**1/2 cup fresh parsley**
**2 tablespoons coarse salt**
**1 tablespoon freshly ground black pepper**
**1 large clove garlic**
**1 can of beer**
**1 chicken, about 4 pounds**

Combine the first 5 ingredients in a food processor and purée to make a paste. Massage it into the chicken, taking extra care to work the mixture under the skin (because the bird will be vertical, some of the seasonings on the outside of the skin will fall off).

Start the grill and warm it until it is about 350 degrees in the cooking chamber. If you are using a gas grill, once it has come up to temperature, turn off all but one of the burners. If you are using charcoal, be sure all the coals have been raked to one side or arranged around the periphery. Using the hand test, the grate will be hot enough when you can hold your palm 5 inches above it for no more than 5 seconds.

Pour out (or drink) half of the beer. Place the half-full can on a cast-iron skillet (or use a disposable aluminum pan), then prop the chicken up on it by inserting the can into the body cavity. The two legs, untrussed or untucked, and the can should form a tripod.

Place the skillet with the beer-can chicken on the cool side of the grill, set the cover in place and allow it to cook for roughly 1 1/2–2 hours, making sure the temperature of the cooking chamber stays between 300 and 400 degrees F (350 degrees F is the ideal). If you are using a charcoal grill, position the opened lid vents so they are on the same side as the chicken. If the lid won't close (meaning your chicken is too tall), arrange the lid so that the side containing the coals is sealed, and the side beside the meat is ajar. In the event you have to do this, close the lid vents completely to retain more heat, if necessary. The chicken is ready when the internal meat temperature is 165 degrees F.

ALTERNATIVELY, skip the beer can and skewer the whole bird on the spit. Arrange the flames so they run on either side of where the chicken will turn on your rotisserie. Place a drip pan underneath, cover the grill, and allow the meat to cook 1 1/2–2 hours, keeping the cooking chamber around 350 degrees.

---

### SEASONING CHICKEN

Filled with flavor, fat-soluble vitamins and antimicrobial fatty acids, chicken skin is extremely tasty and good for you. It also helps to protect the meat of the bird and keeps it juicy, even when cooked at high temperatures. However, this miraculous skin makes seasoning poultry a bit of a challenge. If you only season the surface of the skin, little of the flavorings penetrate through to the meat. Pastured chicken is so flavorful that the meat will taste excellent on its own, but if you're going to the effort of adding herbs and spices, it would be nice to taste them throughout the meat. Thus, here are a few tips for seasoning your poultry.

If cooking the bird whole, use the cavity. Herbs, garlic, citrus wedges or spices added to the cavity of the bird will infuse the meat as it cooks in the oven or on the grill.

Season *under* the skin. To do this, slide your fingers along the breast, gently breaking the membrane that holds the skin to the muscle. Next, slide your hand under the skin down over the thighs, drumsticks, and across to the back. Go slowly and do your best not to tear the skin. Then, run your hands under the skin once more, this time massaging the spice rub or paste into the surface of the meat. Once this is done, I always make a point of going back and seasoning the surface of the skin as well, as it is my favorite part of the bird. It's my daughter's, too. She and I have been known to eat the entire skin off a chicken before even bringing it to the table!

---

# Lemon Grill-Roasted Butterflied (or not) Chicken

I first tasted this chicken at the home of Ester Zeroleni and Toto Dalzotto, in Entre Rios, a rural province of Argentina. We had just spent the early evening swimming in the Uruguay River, then walked back to their little farm, watching the cattle graze among the eucalyptus and citrus trees as the sun set. Toto cooked the chicken on a grate above a ring of coals drawn from a separate fire; propped above the chicken was a piece of sheet metal on which burning coals were piled, creating a sort of open oven that roasted the meat. What a treat it was to watch our daughter and her new Argentine playmates tumble about the lawn and scramble after giant toads while we sat by the fire and listened to crickets. I can't taste this recipe without instantly returning to that perfect evening. I've given instructions for butterflying the meat and cooking it over the grill, but it also works well on the rotisserie.

*Good for company*
*Kid-friendly*
*On a budget*
*Serves 4*

**1 whole lemon, cut in half**
**1 tablespoon coarse salt**
**2 teaspoons fresh ground pepper**
**1 tablespoon Herbes de Provence**
**Salmeura, p. 50**
**1 chicken, 3–5 pounds**

To butterfly the chicken:
Set the bird on the counter in front of you, breast-side down, with the hind end facing you. With a set of poultry shears, cut down the entire length of the backbone on one side. Spin the bird around (breast-side still facing down) so that the neck end is now closest to you, then cut along the other side of the backbone and

remove it. Flip the chicken so it is breast-side up. Lay both hands on top of the breast and push down firmly, flattening the roast.

Combine the salt, pepper and Herbes de Provence in a small dish. Mix well. Loosen the skin of the bird and massage half the mixture directly into the meat. Squeeze the juice of the whole lemon over the surface of the bird, then sprinkle the skin with the remaining herb mix.

Light one side of the grill so that the fire is at a medium temperature. You should be able to hold your hand five inches above the grate for five seconds. Scrape the grate clean with a wire brush, then wipe it down with a light coating of olive oil. Lay the bird over the hottest part of the grill and leave the lid off. Sear the bird for no more than two minutes per side, making sure the skin doesn't burn.

Move the chicken to the cool side of the grill, the breast facing up. If you wish to capture the juices, set the bird in a cast-iron skillet or place a drip pan beneath it. Insert a meat thermometer into the thigh or breast, then cover the grill.

Allow the meat to roast about 40–60 minutes, until the internal temperature reads 160–165 degrees. During this time be sure to monitor the temperature of the cooking chamber, adding coals or adjusting the flame as necessary to keep the temperature between 350 and 400 degrees. Allow the meat to rest 5–10 minutes before serving. Warm up the salmeura and pass it with the meat, allowing people to add extra seasoning as they choose. Serve this dish with fresh greens, summer tomatoes and *Ensalada de Papas y Huevos* (recipe follows).

ALTERNATIVELY, don't butterfly the bird. Season the meat as directed above, then arrange the flames on your grill so they run on either side of where the chicken will turn on your rotisserie. Place a drip pan underneath, cover the grill, and allow the meat to cook 1 1/2–2 hours, keeping the cooking chamber around 350 degrees.

# ENSALADA DE PAPAS Y HUEVOS
## (Potato Egg Salad)

Ester served this simple potato salad alongside the lemon chicken that steamy night in Entre Rios. The salty tartness quickly became a favorite in our family and a welcome variation on our standard potato and mayonnaise salad.

> 1 pound boiling potatoes, cut up
> 4 eggs, hard boiled, peeled and diced
> 1–2 teaspoons salt
> 1 teaspoon black pepper
> 4 tablespoons red wine vinegar
> 1/2 cup olive oil

Put the potatoes in a pot of water and boil until they are tender but not mushy, about 30 minutes. Drain them and allow them to cool to room temperature. Cut up the cooked potatoes and place in a large bowl. Add the eggs, olive oil, salt, pepper and vinegar. Stir well. Add additional salt and vinegar to taste. Serve immediately or chill 1–2 hours in the refrigerator.

## CHICKEN HYGIENE

When working with raw meat, especially poultry, hygiene is critical. The following guidelines might seem intimidating if you are new to cooking, but they will quickly become second-nature.

1. Always wash your hands with soapy water immediately after handling raw meat. When cooking an entire meal with vegetables, starches and meat, it is wise to wash your hands several times during the process.

2. With each round in the kitchen or on the grill, devote a set of cutting boards, platters, knives and other necessary utensils *exclusively* to the raw cause. Use them only for working with the raw meat, then wash the utensils thoroughly in hot soapy water afterward. And don't forget about any dishtowels or potholders that might have slid up against the meat! Be sure to toss them in the laundry.

3. When the meat is cooked, use a clean set of platters, cutting boards and utensils for removing it from the grill, carving and serving.

4. It should go without saying, but be sure that you don't use cutting boards and knives that have touched the raw meat on your vegetables or other foods—especially if they will be served raw, such as in salads.

# POUSSIN À LA MOUTARDE
## (Chicken with Mustard Glaze)

Here's a lovely rotisserie recipe I learned during our travels in France. If you don't have a rotisserie, use the indirect method.

*Elegant*
*Good for company*
*On a budget*
*Serves 4*

**1 clove garlic, peeled**
**1/4-1/3 cup Dijon mustard (extra if your bird is large)**
**1/2 cup sour cream**
**2 tablespoons butter**
**salt and freshly ground pepper, to taste**
**1 chicken, 3–5 pounds**

Insert the clove of garlic in the cavity of the chicken. Rub the mustard underneath the skin and over the surface of the bird. The chicken should be coated with a thick layer when you're finished. Sprinkle the skin generously with salt and pepper.

Set up the grill for cooking with a rotisserie. If using charcoal, arrange the coals in two rows on either side of where the chicken will be rotating. If using gas, turn on the front and rear burners. Place a drip pan or cast-iron skillet just below where the bird will be.

Put the chicken on the spit and allow it to cook with the cover in place about 1 1/2–2 hours, maintaining the temperature of your cooking chamber around 350 degrees. The meat is cooked when an internal meat thermometer in the thigh reads 160-165 degrees. Do not remove it from the grill yet.

INDIRECT METHOD: Build a fire on one side of the grill. Put the lid down and allow the cooking chamber to come up to 350 degrees. Season the chicken as directed above, then lay it breast-side up in a cast-iron skillet and set it on the cool side of the grate.

Cover the grill and allow the meat to roast 1 1/2–2 hours, until the meat thermometer in the thigh registers 160-165 degrees. Do not remove it from the grill yet.

Once the chicken is cooked, gently warm the sour cream in a small pan over low heat on your kitchen stove. When the cream has turned to liquid, brush it on the surface of the bird, allowing any surplus mustard to fall away. Allow the chicken to cook 10 minutes longer.

Remove the chicken from the grill and allow any accumulated juices in the cavity to pour into the drip pan or skillet. Set the chicken on a cutting board and allow it to rest 5-10 minutes. Add the butter to the pan juices and simmer the mixture on the stove top or over your grill flames until the butter melts. Add additional salt and pepper to taste and serve with the chicken once it has been carved.

Ok, ok, I bashed this practice at the beginning of the chapter. But the truth is, no matter what I say, there are a few of us who are still going to grill chicken parts. Here's a little guide and some recipe suggestions to help you through the process.

*To Cut Up a Chicken*

Arrange the bird so that it is breast-side up, with the cavity facing you. Lift it by one leg, causing the skin between the thigh and the body to grow very taut. Slice through this tight skin with a good chef's knife.

Hoist the bird even further while holding onto the leg, until you can feel the ball of the thigh rotate in the "hip socket." Grabbing the bird with both hands, pop the ball out of the socket.

Using your knife, work your way through the remaining bone, membrane, meat and skin beneath the socket, freeing the leg from the body.

With the leg cut free, notice the line of fat that divides the thigh from the drumstick. Cut through the joint between the lower leg and thigh at this line.

Repeat steps 1–4 with the other leg of the bird.

Flip the bird over so that it is breast-side down. Pull the wing away from the body and cut the joint that holds it to the breast. If you like, slice diagonally and make the cut a little farther onto the breast so that a bit of breast meat is included with the wing. Repeat for the other side.

Flip the bird so that it is lying sideways. Find the rib cage. Using poultry shears, cut through the ribs on each side, separating the breasts from the backbone.

Lay the breasts, meat-side up, on the cutting board. Using your knife and a good amount of thrust, chop through the breastbone, dividing the breasts into two halves.

*Cooking Chicken Parts*

Light the grill and close the lid, allowing the heat to build up for about 5 minutes. When the grill is ready, you should be able to hold your hand 5 inches above the grate for no more than 5 seconds. If using a gas grill, leave one burner on high and turn off the others. If using charcoal, be sure all the coals are raked over to one side of the grill.

Scrape the grate clean with a wire brush, then oil it lightly.

To cook the thighs and legs: Sear the thighs and legs 1–2 minutes per side (with the lid up), directly over the hot part of the grill, then move them to the cool side. Cover and grill, without turning, for about 15 minutes. If the thighs and legs are not separated, allow them to cook on the indirect heat for 18–20 minutes. When they are done, the juices will run clear.

To grill the breasts: Assuming your breasts are bone-in, sear them directly over the flame for 2–3 minutes, then promptly move them to the cool part of the grill and continue cooking for another 15 minutes.

To grill the wings: Do the reverse that you would for the legs and breasts. Start the wings on the cool side of the grill. Allow them to cook there, with the lid on, for about 6–8 minutes, without turning. Then move them to the hot side and finish them directly over the flame, about 2 minutes per side, until the skin is deep golden brown and crispy.

*Seasoning Your Cut-up Chicken:*
There are a number of recipes throughout this book that work wonderfully when cooking chicken parts:

- Lemon Grill-Roasted Chicken, p. 139
- Poussin à la Moutard, p. 143
- Mediterranean Marinade, p. 109 (from Mediterranean-Style Pork Kebabs)
- Ginger-Lime Marinade, p. 104 (from Ginger-Lime Pork Chops)
- Coffee-Allspice Jerk Paste, p. 116
- Lemon-Garlic Marinade, p. 95

# CURRIED CHICKEN SALAD

This chicken salad is so easy and tasty, I find myself making it year-round. Kids love it, it stores well, and it makes terrific chicken salad sandwiches.

*Minimal preparation*
*Kid-friendly*
*On a budget*
*Serves 4*

**2 cups grilled chicken, diced**
**1/2 cup raisins**
**1/2 cup dried cranberries**
**1 cup salted cashews**
**2 ribs celery, diced**
**3 tablespoons curry powder**
**1 tablespoon turmeric**
**3/4 cup mayonnaise**
**6 cups salad greens**
**1/2 cup olive oil**
**2 tablespoons lemon juice**
**salt and pepper to taste**

Combine the chicken, raisins, dried cranberries, cashews and celery in a large bowl. Add the curry powder and turmeric and stir well, then add mayonnaise. Stir well once more, then add salt and pepper to taste. If you have the time, refrigerate the salad 2 hours or overnight. The flavors will meld and taste better, but you can serve it immediately if you're pressed for time.

Rinse the salad greens and pour them in a separate bowl. Whisk together the olive oil, lemon juice, and a pinch of salt and pepper. Pour the dressing on top of the greens and toss until they are well-coated.

Arrange the salad greens on four dishes or in shallow bowls. Top with the chicken salad and serve.

# CHICKEN, WALNUT AND WILD RICE SALAD

In our house, we often find ourselves with leftover wild rice at the same time we have leftover chicken. This breezy dish makes use of both.

*Minimal preparation*
*On a budget*
*Serves 4*

**2 cups grilled chicken, diced**
**2 cups wild rice or wild rice blend, cooked and**
    **chilled**
**2–3 carrots, finely diced**
**2 celery ribs, split in half and finely sliced**
**1 bell pepper, diced**
**1 small red onion, finely chopped**
**1 cup walnuts, coarsely chopped**
**1 batch Mustard Vinaigrette (p. 149)**

Toss all the salad ingredients into a large bowl. Pour on the vinaigrette and toss well to coat the greens. Serve immediately.

# MUSTARD VINAIGRETTE

**1/2 cup olive oil**
**1/4 cup cider vinegar**
**2 tablespoons Dijon mustard**
**1/2 teaspoon salt**
**1/2 teaspoon ground black pepper**

Add all the above ingredients to a small bowl. Whisk well until the dressing emulsifies.

---

## GRILL GARDENING

Before I sold our meat at a farmers' market with wonderful organic vegetable growers, I used to grow all our own vegetables. Now, with the chaos of kids, farm and work, it is nice to rely on my neighbors at the Saturday market for a steady supply of tasty summer veggies. Still, I have a special garden flanking my Weber. I call it my grill garden, and in it I grow everything I need for a season of cookouts. The perennial bed has patches of mint, chives and thyme that are frequently called into seasoning service. On the deck I have cherry tomatoes growing in pots, great for skewering—and for amusing hungry toddlers. Also in pots I keep oregano, parsley, sage, dill, cilantro, basil, tarragon…any herb I can think of that might dress up my meat before it hits the embers. Just outside my kitchen door I can snag the fresh herbs easily for any meal. My favorite cookout herb, however, is a lovely lemon verbena plant, which I learned to cherish on steamy asado nights down in Argentina. Graciela, my host, taught me how to make the best lemon verbena tea, which is a most refreshing accompaniment to any meat off the coals:

*Lemon Verbena Tea*
2 stems lemon verbena
1 whole lemon
2 quarts water
honey, to taste

Boil the lemon verbena in the two quarts of water for about three minutes. Squeeze in the juice of the lemon, then add enough honey to please your palate. Refrigerate for several hours and serve cold. For additional flavor, add another sprig of verbena to the jar of tea as it chills.

# Asian-Style Chicken Salad

This one is not only high-fiber and healthy, but it tastes good, too. My daughter loved it.

*Good for company*
*Kid-friendly*
*Minimal preparation*
*On a budget*
*Serves 4*

**2 cups grilled chicken, diced (or more, if you**
**have extra)**
**2 cups green or red cabbage, coarsely shredded**
**1 cucumber, peeled, seeded and finely chopped**
**2 carrots, shredded**
**1 cup salted peanuts or cashews**
**Sesame-Ginger Vinaigrette (p. 151)**

Toss all the salad ingredients into a large bowl. Pour the vinaigrette on top, then stir well to coat. Serve immediately, or chill 1 hour before eating.

# Sesame-Ginger Vinaigrette

3 tablespoons toasted sesame oil
3 tablespoons sunflower oil
1/4 cup rice vinegar
2 tablespoons tamari
1/2 cup fresh mint, finely chopped
1/2 cup chives or green onions, minced
2 teaspoons fresh ginger, grated
2 tablespoons Dijon mustard
1/4 teaspoon cayenne pepper

Combine all the above ingredients in a glass bowl. Whisk well until the dressing emulsifies.

# WHAT MAKES GOOD FOOD?

Any cookbook can rattle off ingredients and techniques for cooking good food. We can draw culinary inspiration from all corners of the world—from China, India, Argentina, the American South, France. Every country, and every region of every country, has culinary masters with something to teach us. And whether we're rank beginners charring our first steak over the coals, or savvy masters informed in all the gastronomic traditions, there is always something more to learn.

But no matter how many cookbooks we buy, and no matter how many recipes we read, there are still only a few concepts that we need to understand in order to prepare great food. Follow the principles for the best food, and no matter how novice or advanced your kitchen and grilling experience, the results will be delicious.

*The best food* comes from farmers who love what they do. The best food is the result of careful loving stewardship between the farmer, his crops and livestock, and his land. The best food has flavor that will vary from plant to plant, from farm to farm, from season to season, and from animal to animal.

*The best food* is purchased by people who care about their families and loved ones, who will buy directly from the producer, who verify the source and the growing practices, and who will handle the food with love, devotion and respect in the kitchen. The best food is cooked in the home and given the time it deserves. The best food is not acquired pre-cooked and pre-wrapped after being shipped thousands of miles.

*The best food* is enjoyed at the table in a spirit of appreciation, love and conviviality. The television is off, e-mail is shut down, the phone is off the hook. It is a time when loved ones put aside daily stresses and pressures and come together to talk, to taste, and to celebrate life.

*The best food* drains no resources from our planet. It cycles and restores them. The best food does not require wars for oil, water or land, but instead fosters peace brought on by plentitude. The best food does not drain our energy as we prepare it, but instead replenishes energy by nourishing our bodies, our communities and our souls.

If you take nothing else away from this book, take away just this thought: Settle for nothing but the best. *Bon appétit.*

CHAPTER SIX

# Culinary Notes from Argentina

## —And Tips for Cooking with a Parilla

With the exception of urban residents who must make do with restaurant asados or get by with tiny portable grills on their apartment balconies, no home in Argentina is complete without its *quincho*, an outdoor kitchen/dining area, the center of which is the *parilla*. Typically, the parilla is a brick or tile hearth with a grate that rests roughly 12 inches above the hearth floor. In its more rudimentary forms, it is simply a metal grate propped up on cinder blocks or bricks and surrounded by scrap sheet metal on a patch of burned-out grass. Both work well and are handled the same way. A fire is first built under the grate, then later moved to the back corner of the hearth, leaving only a small bed of embers behind. Throughout the cooking process, the asador feeds the fire with hardwood. As the wood cooks down, the glowing embers are then shoveled underneath the grate, where the meat roasts. In most cases the embers are monitored to keep the roasting temperature on the grill around 300 degrees. The asador controls this temperature by the amount of embers in the pile. More embers raise the temperature; fewer cool it.

Among the tourists who visit within her borders, Argentina has a reputation for wonderful steak; however, while living in Argentina and visiting local families, we learned that the quintessential asado fare was *costillas,* or beef short ribs. In fact, costillas are so much a part of this country's grilling tradition that to order an "asado" in a restaurant means that short ribs will be brought to the table.

Many people, myself included, tend to like their meat well-seared and caramelized on the outside, and pink or blood-rare on the inside. However, short ribs off the grill need to be treated differently. Here in North America, we assume that short ribs should be braised. We would never dream of cooking them in the dry heat of a fire. However, when grilled slowly and thoroughly so that the meat is evenly roasted throughout, showing only a trace of pink, these short ribs are more beefy and delicious than any steak I've ever feasted upon. Yes, unlike a piece of filet mignon, they require a steak knife to eat, but they are nowhere near as chewy as you might imagine and they are unbelievably delicious.

Before traveling down to the mecca of tango and beef, I'd read about two famous Argentine seasonings for meat: chimichurri and salsa criolla, piquant sauces featuring various mixtures of raw onions, red peppers, tomatoes, vinegar, paprika, fresh garlic and herbs. American food magazines rhapsodize about these pungent concoctions, claiming they are the secret to great Argentinean beef. That's a bunch of bull (no pun intended). I sampled a lot of meat at home grills and a lot of meat from restaurant grills—both good restaurants, and lousy restaurants. Any time chimichurri or salsa criolla were brought to the table, a red flag went up. Inevitably, the meat being presented would have been unskillfully grilled, usually done too fast so that the flavor profile had not fully developed. Also, quite often, I discovered that the sauces were used as a cover-up for meat that was bordering on rancidity. The presence of the chimichurri or salsa criolla on the table almost always forecasted a bout of gastro-enteritis for our family. Except on very rare occasions, the most skilled grill masters never used these concoctions. Instead, they relied on quality beef selections, patient cooking, and salt alone or a simple salt-pepper-garlic solution, or *salmeura* (a salt-saturated garlic water explained on page 50).

Still, chimichurri or salsa criolla can be fun accompaniments to grilled pork or beef, although I find they taste far better on good tortilla chips. I was awarded a number of recipes from the archives of the families that hosted us during our South American travels, and I have included two on pages 54–55.

Beef was definitely the star of the Argentinean grill. But while traveling and studying grill techniques down there, I learned about grilling chicken, rabbit, pork, fish, lamb and vegetables. Throughout the book I've translated the meat recipes I learned into techniques that work on American grills and, for the most part, we can achieve very similar results in this country, provided we are cooking with good-quality charwood, and not charcoal briquettes. The recipes will also work with gas grills, but the flavor will not be quite as interesting as what can be produced from charwood. For explanations about the differences between charwood, charcoal briquettes and gas, see chapter one.

For those of you who have already gone ahead and constructed your own parillas, most of the recipes in this book translate very easily. Here are the general guidelines for using your parilla with this book:

> Set the grate in place.
>
> Build a small fire underneath the grate. Allow it to flame up and thoroughly heat the grill.
>
> Once the fire has produced 2–3 handfuls of embers, use a shovel to swiftly move the wood and flames to the back corner of the parilla, out of the area where your meat will cook, leaving the embers behind. This will be a little tricky at first, but with practice you will soon be able to shift it with one swift motion.
>
> Using a metal rake or barbecue tongs, arrange the remaining embers into an even bed.
>
> Hold your hand directly at the grate, at the same level where the meat will cook. For cooking short ribs, legs of lamb, chicken, pork ribs, lamb ribs, sausages or any roasts, you should be able to hold your hand at the grate, at the same level as the meat, for 8 seconds (take care not to burn yourself). If you have a thermometer, the temperature at the grate should be about 300 degrees. If you are cooking

steaks, chops or kebabs, you'll want the embers to be considerably hotter to accomplish the quick sear. For steaks and chops, you'll also need to keep a cooler spot on the grill for bringing the meat up to temperature once it has been seared (or be prepared to shovel some of the embers away to cool the grate).

Lay your meat on the grill, always bone-side down. Allow the majority of the cooking to take place with the bones facing the embers. The theory here is to allow the embers to heat the bones, then for the bones to cook the meat. Only when the meat is nearly cooked should you turn it to sear the remaining sides.

Monitor your fire constantly. Keep feeding it, as you will need to constantly be generating new embers to shovel under the grate.

I found cooking with a parilla to be tantamount to a meditation...even better, in fact. It requires the asador's complete attention, as he or she must constantly monitor the fire, the embers, the temperature at the grate. You will be able to think of little else. Because it is an open-hearth style of cooking, the asador also has the rare task of watching the meat as it cooks. Very often in this country, we have a tendency to turn our heads while the miraculous biochemical actions take place that turn meat from raw flesh to feast. As you work with your parilla, you will come to know, feel, smell and see the various transformations that happen during this process. You will notice how the raw muscle sweats, then slowly caramelizes, then contracts and pulls away from the bone. In very short order you will be able to do mixed grills far more easily than you can with American grills, as you will find you have much more control over temperature when you work with the embers. You will be able to create hot spots, cool spots, and mid-range cooking areas. And you, too, will become a master asador (or asadora)!

# INDEX

# Recipe Index

# Also by Shannon Hayes:

## *The Grassfed Gourmet Cookbook*

### *Healthy Cooking & Good Living with Pasture-Raised Foods*

- A definitive guide to the health, animal welfare, environmental, and culinary benefits of grass-fed foods.
- Simple strategies for finding, preparing, and cooking pasture-based foods as well as techniques for getting the most out of your purchases.
- More than 125 delicious recipes by some of today's best pasture-based farmers, featuring beef, lamb, pork, venison, bison, goat, veal, poultry, rabbit and dairy products.
- Countless tools to help farmers market their products, including cutting instructions, explanations for consumers who choose to buy whole, half and quarter animals, and easy-to-read reference charts matching all the cuts on an animal with the appropriate cooking methods.

"Finally. A cookbook that does justice to the superb quality of the meat, eggs, and dairy products from grass-fed animals. Shannon Hayes takes the mystery out of cooking products from pastured animals. Once you've read her book, you, too, will be a 'grass-fed gourmet.'"—Jo Robinson, author of *Pasture Perfect*, coauthor of *The Omega Diet*, creator of www.eatwild.com.

"*The Grassfed Gourmet Cookbook* is a required companion for all of us who wish to enjoy these foods and support a better way of farming and eating."—Bruce Aidells, author of *The Complete Meat Cookbook*.

# Order your copies of *The Farmer and the Grill* and *The Grassfed Gourmet* today!

To order online, go to www.grassfedcooking.com.
Mail orders to:
Shannon Hayes, 270 Rossman Valley Road, Richmondville, NY 12149

_____ Yes! Please send me 1 copy of *The Grassfed Gourmet Cookbook*. I have enclosed a check or money order for $25.98 ($22.95 for the book, plus $3.03 for shipping and handling).

_____ I would like two or more copies of *The Grassfed Gourmet Cookbook*. I have enclosed $22.95 for each copy, and understand that, as part of this special offer, shipping and handling charges will be waived.  Please send me _____ # copies.

_____ Please send me 1 copy of *The Farmer and the Grill*. I have enclosed a check or money order for $20.50 ($17.95 for the book, plus $2.55 for shipping and handling).

_____ Please send me two or more copies of *The Farmer and the Grill*. I have enclosed $17.95 for each copy, and understand that, as part of this special offer, shipping and handling charges will be waived. Please send me _____ # copies.

_____ One of Each special: Please send one copy each of *The Farmer and the Grill* and *The Grassfed Gourmet Cookbook*, for $40.90. As part of this special offer, shipping and handling charges will be waived.

SHIP TO: Name _____
Address _____
City_____ State _____ Zip _____
Phone_____ email _____
    Total amount for books:                _____
    Total shipping (if applicable):      _____
    Subtotal books and shipping       _____
    NYS residents, please add 8% sales tax:  _____
    Total amount enclosed:              _____

___ I have included a check or money order drawn on a U.S. bank account for the above amount. *Please make checks payable to Shannon Hayes.*

___ Please charge my Mastercard or Visa.
My credit card number _____. Expiration date:_____.
I agree to pay the above amount in full subject to and in accordance with the agreement governing the use of this card.
_____ Signature

Photo by Teri Currie

ABOUT THE AUTHOR:

Shannon Hayes writes and works with her family on Sap Bush Hollow Farm in upstate New York, where they raise pastured livestock. She holds a Ph.D. in sustainable agriculture and community development from Cornell, and a B.A. in Creative Writing from Binghamton University. She is the author of *The Grassfed Gourmet*, and *The Farmer and the Grill*, as well as numerous articles and essays on food, farming and rural living. To contact the author or learn more, visit www.shannonhayes.info. To learn more about Sap Bush Hollow Farm, visit www.sapbush.com.

ABOUT THE ILLUSTRATOR:

Bob Hooper was completely unaware that, when he asked Shannon Hayes to marry him, he would be sentenced to a lifetime of drawing livestock cartoons, processing chickens, and testing recipes. Nevertheless, he enjoys his livelihood with the family farm, and finds periodic amusement as a freelance illustrator, basket weaver, diaper changer and devoted daddy.